Touch the Dragon

Touch the Dragon
A Thai Journal

Karen Connelly

Turnstone Press

Turnstone Press
607–100 Arthur Street
Winnipeg, Manitoba
Canada R3B 1H3
www.TurnstonePress.com

Turnstone Press gratefully acknowledges the assistance of the
Canada Council for the Arts and the Manitoba Arts Council.

Cover design: Doowah Design

Cover photograph: Karen Connelly

Text design: Manuela Dias

This book was printed and bound in Canada by
Hignell Printing for Turnstone Press.

Second printing: May 1993
Third printing: November 1993
Fourth printing: December 1993
Fifth printing: January 1994
Sixth printing: May 1994
Seventh printing: November 1995
Eighth printing: October 1998

Canadian Cataloguing in Publication Data

Connelly, Karen, 1969–

Touch the dragon

ISBN 0-88801-162-8

1. Thailand - Description and travel - 1976 -
2. Connelly, Karen, 1969– - Diaries.
3. Connelly, Karen, 1969–   - Journeys -
Thailand. I. Title.

DS566.2.C65 1992   915.9304'44   C92-098128-3

*This book is for the people of Thailand, especially
Ajahn Champa, Goong and Meh Dang.*
Cop koon muc muc ka.

We have forgotten that once—if only once—we saw the world before us: whole and green and alive with promise.

—Timothy Findley
Inside Memory

Perhaps things are most beautiful when they are not quite real; when you look upon a scene as an outsider, and come to possess it in its entirety and forever; when you live the present with the lucidity and feeling of memory; when, for want of connection, the world deepens and becomes art.

—Mark Helprin
"Tamar"

Preface

IN 1985, AT THE AGE OF SIXTEEN, I was painfully bored with high school and hungry for living knowledge of the world. After years of reading *National Geographic* and the likes of Isak Dinesen and Rudyard Kipling, I knew stunning places existed beyond the one I lived in. Calgary's marvels had grown tame for me. Impatient to see what I was missing, I applied to the Rotary Exchange Program, hoping to escape from Canada and go very far away. After I filled in many forms and convinced a selection committee of my responsible nature, my wish came true. In August of 1986, I left Canada with three large pieces of luggage which contained a few clothes, many books, and a great deal of liquorice and paper. The ants devoured the liquorice in my first weeks there, but the paper survived.

Touch the Dragon took over five years and four countries to become a book. I wrote the raw bulk of it in Denchai, sifted through hundreds of letters and journal entries in Canada, compiled and rewrote them in Spain, worked on the manuscript again in Canada, and edited it in France. Through those years and countries, I became more and more surprised at the young woman who'd lived in Asia and written with such unabashed enthusiasm about her world there. I doubt I'm flexible enough now to accept the conditions and rules I did then, but at seventeen, I was a passionate initiate in a country which became more real and more beautiful the longer I stayed. My true education began there and, in many ways, I consider it the country of my birth. Thailand opened the world and this book tries to describe what that was like. Of course, it falls short—it is not equal to the experience itself—but it is an attempt, a record of living in a place that awakened every possibility of growth in me. I hope *Touch the Dragon* conveys the *reality* of such possibilities to those who read it.

Thailand came to me like a gift; with this book I mean to say *thank you.*

Lesvos, Greece
June 1992

Acknowledgements

I would like to express sincere thanks to the following people and organizations: The Calgary Centennial Rotary Club; Lorne Plantje, who suggested I escape; Jorge Romberg, *con un abrazo muy fuerte;* Rod Turnbull, who endured me; The Rotary Club of Denchai and all my Thai fathers; Rotary International; my Thai families; the former Alberta Foundation for Literary Arts, who funded this book when it was still just an embryo; Christine Cook and Jackie Henry, who read and often inspired the first words; Timothy Findley, Nancy Holmes and Leslie Bell, for their generous encouragement and criticism. I also thank Pat Sanders for her work on the manuscript, her patience and her postal acrobatics.

Brief excerpts of this book appeared in *blue buffalo.*

August 21, 1986

LEAVING CANADA. A view of the body of mountains: deep
sockets of aquamarine, blue veins slipping over cliff-sides,
stone edges splintering from the earth like cracked bones.

When I think of the span of countries, when I run my
fingers over the skin of a map, I get dizzy. I am too high up
now—I should have glided into this journey on a boat. As
the country pulls out from under me, I overturn like a glass
on a yanked table-cloth, I spill. Land steadies people, holds
them, even if they imagine they control it. Land owns and
defines us. Without it, we become something else.

After refuelling in Kyoto, we are moving again, rising
into another time zone, another time. These are the first
pages of a new country. There's almost nothing to write yet
because I know so little. I can't even imagine where I'm
going. I am utterly alone, a small bit of dust blown into Asia's
deep green eye. I lean against the glass and gaze down at an
emerald flood, knowing I'll never be able to soak up such
radiance. It's a colour I never knew I'd see, the astonishing
canvas of a dream, undreamed.

At the airport in Bangkok, a bald foreigner lugs three

gallons of water on his shoulder. He explains to suspicious customs officials that he has brought water from home because the water here is unsafe. There is laughter, a waving of dark arms and pale palms. I stumble through customs, crippled by luggage and jet lag. One English word rings out: taxi. The world is a wet braid of heat and flesh, glimpses of gold-studded teeth, shirts open to shining bellies, purple tattoos, wreaths of jasmine. Above the horde of cab-drivers looms a hand-painted sign warning all tourists to beware of thieves, illicit business deals, drugs and fake gems. The air slides over me thick as honey. I have never felt such tropical warmth before.

Then I see a cardboard sign with my name on it bobbing up in the crowd. Someone has come to get me. Someone has come to take me (farther) away.

August 22

WE ARE DRIVING northwards under black clouds, through darkness broken by lightning. I could believe now that the earth is flat, and its far edges are sparking flame. Rice fields, tree groves, gleaming oval ponds flash out of the night. Mr. Prasit Piyachinda and Mr. Prasert Jeenanukulwong have both suggested I call them *paw* for the sake of simplicity. Paw Prasit speaks English. "We will treat you like a daughter, and you will treat us like father." The Rotary Club of Denchai has almost twenty members. I can't pronounce any of their names. "You must learn to speak Thai very quickly," Paw Prasit explains. "It will not be difficult. No one in your family speaks English. You have no choice." He turns around to smile at me. He talks about spicy food, a famous Buddhist monk who is also a great fortune-teller, the school I will go to, the people who are anxious to meet me. When I ask why these people want to meet me, he giggles. "Why, because you are a falang." A foreigner. It is my first Thai word.

Sudden light spears the heavy rain. I squint out the

streaming windows. The men laugh at my fascination with the countryside. "Are you afraid of the . . . the . . ."

"The lightning," I finish for Paw Prasit.

"Ah, yes, yes, are you afraid of it? My daughter, yes, is. She will not look at fields at night, fields in rain." He points towards a distant clump of trees and taps at the window. "Dragons. She says they are dragons." He laughs, turns to Prasert, translates, they laugh again, then hoot more at some other joke. I peer through the glass; his daughter is right. There they are, tree-dragons, moulded by wind and shadow, heavy-skulled dinosaurs gathered under lightning at the edges of ponds. They lean down to the water, their scaled flanks gleaming with rain.

I FALL ASLEEP, sliding down onto the seat, listening to Paw Prasit say, "And people will call you falang in the street because at first they will not know your name." I will be the only white person in the town. "You will be popular. Also there is a green fruit in Thailand called falang and when you eat it, everyone will laugh and say, 'Falang eat falang. Hahaha. Ha ha.' " Again he translates for Paw Prasert (why are their names so similar?) and both men slap their knees at this hilarious play on words. I keep missing the jokes in everything, possibly because I'm so tired. What time is it here? What time is it in Canada? Canada? The word sounds funny. I slump down farther on the seat and listen to wheels humming and my guardians speaking Thai. It is indecipherable birdsong. They talk on, their voices climbing and sliding down the banisters of five tones and strange letters. This is not comparable to high school French.

Suddenly, inexplicably, they are standing outside the car and calling me. "Kalen, Kalen, to bathroom now. We are in Phitsanulok. For pee-pee." The door is opened for me. I receive a handful of toilet paper and a gentle push in the right direction. I am disoriented, eyes salted with sleep. The young men hanging about the gas pumps stare and stare.

3

Once I am in the dark little washroom, reality swarms; the pungent odour of urine burns the dreamy quality out of everything. I lose my footing on the wet edges of the Thai toilet and laugh, imagining the embarrassment of breaking my ankle in a toilet the very first day. This is Thailand, the land of smiles, the Venice of the Orient, the pearl of Asia. The travel-agency phrases run off my tongue as mosquitoes settle on my thighs, arms, neck. Are they malarial or harmless? A few dark stains move up and down the walls, and my skin shivers, waiting for invasions.

Walking back across the lot, I notice small reddish lights glowing behind a cage with thin bars. I walk towards them, curious, moving closer, closer, stretching out my hand . . . Paw Prasit yells, "No, no!" but it's too late. All I do is touch the bars and half a dozen gibbons leap shrieking towards my hand.

I scream at their screams, the gas-station attendants come loping across the lot and my Thai fathers rush forward to pull me away. I apologize to everyone. The gibbons are the ones making the fuss. Their furious bodies spring and bounce inside the cage. "You must learn to be careful, Kalen." Paw Prasit takes my arm, his glasses steamed with worry. "There are snakes, too. You know?" He stares at me for a moment, then laughs and says something in Thai, which makes Paw Prasert laugh, too. Even the gas-pumpers giggle and kick a few pebbles, looking up at me even though their heads are lowered. I open the car door and crawl in. When we drive away, the boys wave us off. I stare back at the neon lights of the station for a long time, the savage human faces of the monkeys still vivid in my mind.

WE REACH DENCHAI in the dark, so I see little, other than dogs running through the beams of the headlights, barely making it. We finally stop at the last building on the street. "Liquor store," Paw Prasit says. "This is the liquor store of Paw Prasert. This is where you'll live." Prasert is already out of the car and up on a bench, stretching to press a door buzzer.

As soon as his finger flexes, I hear barking and the rattling slap of a chain. The dog inside the building hurls against the metal door. We wait until the dog begins to whimper, then hear an old man's grunt and sniffle. There's a clatter of keys and a frightening roar of phlegm from the recesses of a throat; finally the door scrapes open along the cement floor. A balding old man beams at us. His skin is the colour and texture of a walnut, he is toothless and he wears nothing but a baggy pair of black satin trousers. Prasit says to me, "Old father is much blind." After awkward introductions, the three of them begin to speak in Thai. I smile and smile. Before coming in with us, the old man shuffles to the road and vigorously spits a small chunk of his lung into the gutter.

Inside the shop, the German shepherd once again begins to bark and strain against her chain. Her lips are pulled back over yellow teeth. Paw Prasert grins proudly, pulls up some long-forgotten vestige of English and yells over the barking, "My dog!" I smile back, nod. Paw Prasit adds, "But no worry, it not hurt you." She leaps toward us again, only to be choked back by the chain. After the old man hits her on the nose, she whimpers and slumps to the ground, chin between her paws. We walk deeper into the liquor store, past piles of dusty crates, a display of Thai whisky, a television, an old desk piled with newspapers and small bags of rice. Each of the men has one of my suitcases and is breathing audibly under its weight, insisting how light it is. We come to a small fridge. Paw Prasert opens it and whispers to Paw Prasit, who turns to me. "He say you take anything you want, you are like a daughter to him. You know?"

Thanking them, I glance into the fridge. It's full of water bottles and a few pots of murky sauces or oil paints.

Up one staircase: bathroom, sister's room, children's room. Paw Prasert's room. The top of another staircase brings us to an uninhabited floor. The one bedroom is for me. "You have room all to self." I am smiling, smiling my thanks. Now the men turn to leave. Yes, yes, see you tomorrow, to begin learning Thai, to begin learning, tomorrow, yes.

And the door closes. I look around: a low bed of cushions, a child's desk, a small mirror, a woven straw chair. Green curtains, green bedspread. A stark naked Thai girl with an erotic smile stares down from a picture on the wall. This smile—she must be kidding—does the trick. I sit on the edge of the bed, hug my elbows and sob for everything that isn't here. I think of the hundreds of days, the thousands of hours I have to stay here. Everything I understand, everything I own is buried in my skull, intangible. I am not feeling particularly brave. I'm sniffling, alone but for a Thai porn queen and three beaten-up suitcases. This does not feel exotic. Around me, the pool of night trembles with crickets and frogs, breaks with the distant bark of dogs, and slowly, slowly, closes over my head.

August 23

IT'S TRUE. I LIVE IN A LIQUOR STORE. Sang Som whisky, Singha beer, crates of it everywhere, hiding the nests of mice. Bottles bang dusty shoulders as Jaree, the servant, heaves them into bright orange trucks. Every time our eyes meet, his face—the face of a beaten boxer, scarred on the eyebrow, the chin—opens into a chipped grin. He leaps up onto the truck and starts tying down crates.

Meh and Pee-Moi, Paw Prasert's sisters, also smile ceaselessly, somewhat in awe of my skin. I am a new life-form to them. Surely they knew about my arrival, but our reactions to so much newness are the same: utter amazement. Pee-Moi, Older Sister Moi, is very anxious about me and follows me around whenever she has a spare moment. She calls me "Sir" because that's all the English she knows. "Yes, Sir, no, Sir, chai, chai." Geway and Noi are Meh's sons, aged eleven and four. The two small boys and the grandparents are the only ones who ignore me. Koon Tah and Koon Yiy, grandfather and grandmother, speak Chinese and spend much of the day watching Chinese soap operas and reading newspapers outside at the stone table. Paw Prasert does not actually live here but twenty kilometres away in Prae, the provincial capital, with his wife and two sons.

I have already forgotten the German shepherd's name, along with the names of ten local children who came to see me this morning. Some of them came literally just to see me, and leaned over the handlebars of their bicycles at a distance, observing, snickering. Others came up the steps and sat with me at the stone table to practise their English. Lin is the one I remember best: tall, very thin, about seventeen, more like a boy than a girl. She stayed with me for hours, naming objects in Thai, repeating them for me while I scratched out phonetic equivalents in English. Thai is so strange a language after English and French. Some of its words begin with "ng" and a single word can have as many as five meanings, depending on the tone. I've been nicknamed, like everyone here. My new name, Ploy, means "gem." Lin tells me the school will have a formal Thai name for me, too, to put on my uniform. (Uniform?) My own name is hard for them to say because all the r's become l's in Thai, and vice versa. In the sounds of Thai, I become Kalen Canary.

I offer Goody liquorice and a display of photographs of Canada to the gathering crowd of neighbours and children. They exclaim over my sister's blonde hair, my young brother ("he bootiful, bootiful"). They want to take home pictures of me to show their parents. I feel like a new acquisition in a famous zoo. There are shrieks of embarrassment and shame at a photo of me standing in shorts and a sleeveless T-shirt. Paw Prasit, who keeps materializing out of nowhere to check on me, grins when he sees the photo. "No good, eh, for Thailand, those clothes. Not nice. But in Roy Gratong festival, you can wear bikini, you know?" I laugh and tell him I don't wear bikinis. When he sees a photo of me in the mountains, working down a cliff with chains and scraped knees, a strange expression takes over his face. He squints at the photo. At first he doesn't believe I am the same girl.

It's been an exhausting but successful first day. I think half my photos are being circulated among the population of Denchai, proclaiming my arrival. The liquorice does not produce the desired reaction, however. It takes me a while to understand, but eventually I realize they love the bright colours of the candies, but the dark centres put them off. Black liquorice bears too great a resemblance to *eug* of *jingjoke*. Lizard shit.

August 27

NAREERAT IS IN THE CENTRE OF PRAE. The school has almost three thousand students, only five hundred of them boys. "It has taken a long time," says Ajahn Champa, "to integrate boys with girls." She is the head of the English department and speaks the language beautifully; it's the first real English I've heard since Japan, and I bask in the familiar sounds. She studied on scholarship in Australia and Britain, and exudes the wisdom of age and experience. Also the scent of lemons. She is spotlessly clean and does not seem to sweat. A drop of salt water regularly gathers at my chin and slides down my neck as if there were a hole in my jaw, but Ajahn Champa's skin is dry and pale gold. She must be near fifty—she tells me she has been teaching for thirty years—but it wouldn't be hard to think she's in her late thirties. What I notice most are her perfect hands and feet, twenty nails precisely sculpted and white-tipped.

She sits down at the long row of tables in the English room and begins to tell me very matter-of-factly what I need to know. As she speaks, fanning her hand open and shut for emphasis, I realize this woman will be my greatest help. She can talk with grace about anything.

—The spicy food will do strange things to my stomach. "Perhaps you are already experiencing that. I have noticed you've been to the bathroom three times since you've arrived."

—My period will probably become irregular because of the change in altitude and temperature.

—Malaria is very unlikely, "unless we put you to work in the rice paddies."

—The children in Nareerat and many of the townspeople will be curious about me; except for the occasional tourist, missionary or Peace Corps member, white people do not appear in Prae. "You may get tired of all the attention, but try not to get upset. They only want to know you."

—I must not touch anyone's head, which is a holy part of the body for Buddhists. "And try to keep your head on a lower level than that of your elders, especially of grandparents, for this is a sign of respect. You will make many mistakes at first, but that is all right. Thais are very tolerant people. But if you make the same mistake over and over, they will think you are very stupid or trying to insult them, so be careful."

—As the head is holy, the feet are unholy, and I have to walk around, not over, objects. It is considered rude to move and touch things or people with your feet. This explains why Meh got all flustered when I pushed the fridge door shut with my toes.

—I must never fail to wear a bra, the eighth deadly sin. "And do not wear make-up or jewellery to school. It is against the rules."

—Making jokes about the Thai Royal Family is unacceptable. "In old Siam, the king and queen were comparable to deities; people could not look at them when they passed through the street. Though it has no political power, the monarchy of today is still highly respected."

—"You will be depressed sometimes. You will long for your country, especially in the first two months. Don't worry, these moments will always pass." She pauses. "Of course, they will always come back. It is not so easy to live in Thailand. It is an old, old place and you come from such a young country. Try to be patient with it, Karen." She is the only Thai I have met so far who can say her English r's.

I spend my first day at school with her. "The seamstress will have your uniform ready in two days. It causes quite an upset to have a student without a uniform." She notices the expression on my face. "Yes, I know, you do not like uniforms, but wait and see. You will soon realize that you are different enough, even in a uniform. It will make you feel much more Thai than you think. If you do not wear a uniform, you will stand out too much, and the students will not treat you the same as they treat each other." Already children appear at the doors, giggling. When they see me walking across the schoolyard, they wave and call, "Falang, falang." Ajahn Champa says, "Once they get used to you and know your name, they won't do that anymore. They will talk to you." Before our serious gentle conversation finishes, she asks me, "Which place is like a dream now, this country or your own?" I'm surprised by her question because it so closely touches my own thoughts. "My own," I say, "though Thailand was a dream until last week." She laughs and nods. "Yes, it's true, isn't it? Things you think are so real become dreams when you go away from them. Thailand will be a dream for you one day, when you go away again. Everything changes so easily. I might have lived in London in another life; it is that distant from me now." She sighs, shakes her head, sips her tea delicately as a cat. All afternoon she's been holding, folding and unfolding a yellow embroidered handkerchief. She gives it to me now. "You will need these, because of the heat." Then we go downstairs to meet the other teachers. I forget all their names immediately.

August 29

10   *A GREAT MANY THINGS* slip into confusion, or slide, or slither. Eternal lizards on ceilings and walls; beetles up the drains at dawn, trapped wetly in the sink; the long black tongues of butterflies into the sweetness of flowers. The butterflies here

are red, blue, green, purple, like butterflies drawn by children, the size of sparrows. After rain, snails as big as my fist slurp across the tops of the stone walls, and their slug cousins, elongated and glistening, slime up to my balcony at night. Always, too, there is saliva slipping out the dog's mouth in silver strings to the floor. She has a shaggy fur coat; both of us tolerate the heat badly. Except in the middle of the night when I wake shivering beneath the ceiling fan, I am always sweating.

The country itself sweats; rainy season isn't over yet. Every pathway is damp, every morning is silk-grey with rain. Lin, her brother Deh and I ride bicycles up and down Yantrakitkosol, Yantrak, Denchai's only major road, laughing at each other when the wheels spray our backs with red mud.

Thai words, too, slip, slide out of my mouth, through my mind, into my notebooks, filling up pages within minutes. I'm learning the seventy-six symbols of the alphabet—*gaw gai, khaw khai, kaw quoot, kaw quai*—which take their names from chickens, eggs, water buffalo, turtles, monks, giants, monkeys. . . . How is it possible for one alphabet to have five representations of the letter K, eight of T, four of S? The calligraphy of the symbols changes, but the alterations in sound are not pronounced enough for my mouth to reproduce. Ajahn Champa laughs as I struggle with *baw bai mai* and *phaw pla*, the tree and fish letters. "Your tongue," she notes, "very easily loses its way." I attempt again and again the tonal difference between *cow jai*, to understand, and *gin cow*, to eat rice. To me, a cow is an animal with a cud. Thais use the questions, "Have you eaten rice yet?" and "Where are you going?" as greetings. "Bai nai? Bai nai?" is a question I hear from everyone, even the rickshaw pedlars in the street. "Where are you going?" they ask, when they *know* I'm on my way to school.

Food is extremely important; the people are insulted if you refuse to eat with them. Sharing is a part of friendship. No matter what it looks like, I try a bit of whatever is offered and just don't ask what I'm eating. I haven't encountered much to throw me, except for the spices. The food is delicious—fried or boiled vegetables, chicken, fish, noodles, everything served with rice and sauces.

Ajahn Champa says the funniest thing on earth is watching a queasy *falang* trying to eat *goong den*, dancing shrimp. The tiny live shrimp are tossed into a bowl in the centre of the table, then doused quickly with a hot shower of spices. The spices poison the creatures, make them leap, flick up in the bowl. While they're still dancing, everyone around the table plunges in with a spoon and eats them live. It is almost a game, trying to get the shrimp into your mouth before they jump off your spoon. She says if you get to them fast enough, you can feel them wriggling down your throat. I know I'm not ready for dancing shrimp (often translated in restaurants as "disco prawn"). I knew I'd have to give up vegetarianism to live in Thailand, but I doubt I'll ever be able to put disco prawns in my mouth. Ajahn Champa says there is no fresher way to eat your seafood.

August 30

I ATTEND MY FIRST ROTARY CLUB MEETING this evening, to be introduced to the people who've sponsored my stay here. They greet me in Thai or elementary English, trying their best to make me feel welcome, laughing to compensate for our inability to communicate with words. After my brief introduction speech, they all clap wildly, though no one but Paw Prasit understands a word I've said. He's the only one who speaks English. The Rotary Club meetings I attended at home are nothing in comparison to the ones in Denchai. In Canada, friendly businessmen assemble in ironed suits to listen to formal discourses given by invited speakers. I went to several morning meetings; we breakfasted on croissants and strawberries and were careful not to spill on the white table-cloth.

In Denchai, the Rotarians get together for supper once a week to do the same thing as their Canadian counterparts, but there are no ties and no table-cloths; they throw their chicken bones on the floor. Dogs come in and scrounge under the table, then trot out again, wagging their tails, jaws already crunching for marrow. Before we sing the national anthem, the president hits a large metal gong; the metallic clang wakes everyone up, though this effect does not last for long. After a few minutes of dry discussion, the snores begin again, or whispers, or even hand-over-mouth laughter. I can't understand a thing yet, but Paw Prasit assures me. "Mai pen lai," he says, which is the famous Thai phrase for "never mind." "If you can eat the food, you can learn the language. No problem. Here, try these." I take a large slimy spoonful of some gelatinous vegetable or seaweed. It is almost transparent and crunchy. Paw Prasit stares at me with a mischievous grin. I think I'm eating sea cucumber. "What are these?" I ask after I've swallowed and taken a long gulp of water.

He bites his lower lip. "They are very good for you. Rich in protein. We eat them every week. They are a favourite dish here."

I smile. "Yes, but what are they?"

He pats his belly. "From fish." I express confusion. "You know? This part," again pats his belly, "out of fish." Fish intestines. I've eaten fish intestines. I take another drink of water. "You don't eat them in Canada?" He is surprised. Now he shoves a plate of large animal guts towards me. These are not disguised like the fish; it's impossible to mistake them for exotic vegetables. They are entrails. I tell him I am honestly full, I couldn't possibly eat another bite. He shrugs his shoulders. "Next time, then, okay?"

"Okay." I watch as he takes his first mouthful. "What are they exactly?"

"Aaah, you want?"

"No, no, but what are they?"

He pats his stomach again. "From cow," he says, and grins.

September 3, 1986

I LIKED THE FOOD before I started throwing it up and running down the stairs to the *hongnam* in shameful desperation, clutching my stomach with white-knuckled fingers. Now I hate the food, even the fragrant warm rice and sweet sauces. I've eaten more rice in the last ten days than I've eaten in my entire life in Canada. I want a piece of brown bread and butter. I hate fish sauce. It smells like a dirty wharf in a bottle.

Today, I hate Thailand generally. The naked girl on my wall makes me sick. The staring eyes, the claps and whistles, the kids standing under my window calling my name, which isn't even my real name, this damn uniform I have to wear to school: all of it is driving me mad! I lied! I have no tolerance at all for living in a different culture. I have no facility for languages and I am viciously narrow-minded. I don't care if it's a wonderful experience. My feet are bound in black patent leather Mary Jane shoes and tiny white socks. I have to wear the thick navy blue skirt and starched white shirt five days a week, eleven hours a day, from seven when I dress to six when I get home. I can't go anywhere alone. Paw Prasert's ten-year-old son has to accompany me on walks down the street to the post office. Lin miraculously appears when I say I'm going to walk across the field behind the house. And Paw Prasit is always materializing out of the wet air to ask where I'm going. "I not want you to get lost," he says, but how can I get lost on one major road? I don't care if they're just looking after me and being kind. All this attention is exhausting.

The truth is, I've been lost since I stepped on the plane in Canada. I don't know what I'm doing here; I've forgotten why I've come. There is so much in Canada going on without me.... I can't even scream in frustration because all of Denchai would come bounding up the stairs to see whatever was wrong with the little *falang*. I've had my taste of Thai culture and it has turned my insides to mush. My period started last week and refuses to stop. I've never lost so much blood in a menstrual cycle in my life. Pee-Moi steals horrified glances at my stained underwear when I hang them to dry on the downstairs rack. Why the grave looks over a few bloodstains? I would not have this problem if tampons existed in Prae, but they are not sold in any of the dark little shops for women. Ajahn Champa tells me that Thai women are afraid to use them: they steal a girl's virginity, or get lost in the body.

Jesus H. Murphy Christ.

And the ants have gotten into my liquorice, as well as into my bed. Bed? You mean that load of bricks thinly wrapped in foam? The ants are everywhere, trailing paths across my walls, floor, desk, fingers. At any given moment, I can find a pale Thai ant on or near my body. Not to mention the beetles and roaches and a grotesque singing lizard called a *tukae* which attacks if you get too close to it.

I must have been mad. I left a man, a family, a bed, English, bagels and normal sit-down toilets to be turned into a child who can't even have tantrums and hide in her room. I have to be nice, and open, and friendly. It's sickening.

15

AJAHN CHAMPA has been teaching me about Buddhism. There are more than 30,000 monasteries in Thailand, and many more simple temples of worship. I've already seen some of these temples on major streets, in the middle of empty fields, half hidden in tree groves. Coloured glass glitters on their walls. During the Buddhist Lent, the rainy season between July and September, the number of monks is about 400,000. For a few months or an entire lifetime, Thai men and some Thai women enter monasteries to study the Buddhist scriptures and the art of meditation. Often before they marry, Thai men enter a monastic order as a time of preparation for their impending responsibilities to a family.

There is a long, high, wooden building beside the grounds of Nareerat. Its terraces are decorated with saffron robes hanging out to dry in the sun. This is Prae's local monastery. When I walk to the post office, young monks whistle out the windows, trying to attract my attention. Ajahn Champa attempts to look serious when I mention them to her. "Try to understand them. They are very young and inquisitive. It doesn't matter if they are monks. First, they are Thai. Sometimes they do not realize what they do."

I think they know exactly what they do. They stare down, hoot, giggle and retreat deftly into the shadows of their classrooms, cooing like pigeons. The only reason they're so brave is because their master is down in the temple; like all children, they show off while the teacher is out. If we weren't separated by a stone wall and three storeys, they'd let me pass in utter silence. In the streets, they fall off the curbs to get out of my way. It's a Buddhist tenet they observe in the presence of all females, even their mothers and sisters. A monk is celibate and must not touch women or money or liquor. Their lowered eyelids flit anxiously when we come towards each other on the twisted, narrow sidewalks of Prae. Sometimes, they cross the street just to avoid being brushed by my blue skirt.

Denchai's monastery is on the town's outskirts, clinging to a hillside of tall sparse trees. Like the monks themselves, the monastery is plain to the point of baldness. Grass grows between the stone-lined paths and the knuckled roots of trees. A cool wind blows here. It's so quiet that Deh says we must turn off the motorcycle and walk to the *sala*; he does not want to disturb the *wat* and its inhabitants. Deh has brought me here to see a special monk. He is Australian and has lived in Thailand for almost ten years.

Under the white-tiled gazebo, I meet the most strange-looking white man I've ever seen. Following Deh's example, I bow down three times, head to floor, in a sign of respect to the elderly monk who is with the Australian. I had conceived the image of a typical Australian as being good-looking, blond with blue eyes, and having a lively Aussie accent. Of course, the Australian is bald, shaven even of eyebrows, which makes his deep grey eyes colour his entire face. His skin has been well protected from the sun and looks bleached. His lips resemble two old scars laid together, rising towards cheekbones set high in a narrow skull. His face is a surprise because it's not like the round Oriental faces I've seen every day for the last couple of weeks. He seems to have lived in high places all his life, looking downwards, blown regularly by a very strong gale. Even his body is craggy, shadowed dark under the ledges of bone. He is dangerously thin. I now understand why the most serious monks do little more than meditate; they cannot possibly have the energy to do much else.

But once we begin talking, I am glad I've come. His voice is comforting. There is very little accent left in it anymore; it is distilled, clean-water English. A smile lightens his sombre features and does not go away. He tells me only his Thai name, which is so long that I immediately forget it. When we talk about learning to live in Thailand, he is very sympathetic. "Yes, I know, but you'll soon forget about the difficulties. The people will become accustomed to you, you to them." I make a face. "No, it's true, I promise you. It is so hard at first, I remember, but then everything becomes so beautiful. Even the things you never notice before. Aie, I can see you don't think so. Trust me. In a few months you won't want to go home."

I can't trust him. He doesn't know the life I've left in Canada. "Don't you ever miss Australia?"

He thinks before answering. He speaks slowly. "Sometimes I miss . . . the sea. I lived on the coast. But the rest? No. No, I don't really miss anything."

"Not your family?"

"No."

Then he casually reads my mind and tells me he's been completely celibate for eight years and doesn't miss sex either. I sigh. Maybe he's one of those people who was born with fewer hormones than the rest of us. Maybe he's just crazy. Eight years! When I seriously think about going for a single year without intimate physical contact, I end up howling into my pillow for at least half an hour. This monk, who can't be a day over thirty-five, looks forward to the rest of his celibate life with the gentle expression of a giraffe.

I blink a few times, frown. There is no way to ask tactfully. "So how do you live like that?"

He leans his head back and chuckles with a deep voice, then turns to the older Thai monk, who also seems to be his teacher, and translates our conversation. Typically, the Thai gurgles, "Haha haha haha," and watches me with shining eyes. The two speak together for a few moments. The Australian turns back to me. "The Ajahn says he is so glad to be old now."

I am offered a glass of water; when the monk leans over the wooden table, I see all the separate tendons in his neck rising into the rigid outline of his jaw. The veins shooting up his wrists are vivid blue, smooth under the light skin. He pours the water very gently, as in a ritual, with a grace which is wholly unconscious. Slowly. He even breathes slowly.

I sip my water while he answers my question. "How can I live like this? Like what? This is a good way to live. The Western mind loves logic and numbers and solutions worked out by computers. There is a constant search outside the self, especially in North America. Studying Buddhism—studying any Oriental religion—shows there are no answers in new cars, sailboats, promotions. The only way to achieve true peace is by learning to still the mind like a pool of water. That is the goal of meditation."

"Isn't there a saying about still water stagnating?"

"But a stilled mind will not stagnate, you know. There is also the cliché that stilled water runs deep. The only reason a mind stagnates is because something from the outside contaminates it." He translates for the wrinkled Ajahn, who in turn nods and touches his hands together, flexing them wide open and shut a few times. The monk continues, "The Buddha was not a god, you see, not in the Christian sense. He was not the creator and destroyer. He was a man who believed people could have power over themselves and escape from suffering if they let the outer world fall away, if they did not cling to things, to events, even to each other."

Outwardly, I'm as calm as the monk, observing the big black ants march over the white tiles. I sip my water, nod. Inside, I am raving. It's impossible to let the world fall away. I believe in gravity, in being held to things, history, other human beings. The monk and I argue about this for a while. He is so detached from the world, its people and tragedies, whereas I feel that all of it is somehow my responsibility. Even if I do little, I must think of everything: Afghanistan, starving children, floods, disappearing rainforests. The monk maintains I should put that energy into my own life and the lives of those close to me; I shouldn't be a compassionate whiner. After talking for over half an hour, I realize he has an excellent answer to every argument. When he stops talking with me to translate for the old monk, the teacher begins to explain something in detail, moving his hands and nodding and sometimes breaking into slow giggles. Young Deh, who has been sitting sternly at my side the whole time, laughs out loud. The Australian translates. "The Ajahn says it is terrible to be young. He wants me to tell you to be careful of the world. It is like keeping chickens. Don't get confused. Take the eggs! Leave the shit behind!"

I laugh at this unexpected metaphor. The old monk's entire face curls upward in a grin; even the place where his eyebrows should be rises up into his forehead, opening his eyes wide. He speaks to the Australian. "He is glad you have understood—he says your laughter shows you understand. You laugh geng." I laugh well. The seriousness of the conversation has disappeared. We drink more water and comment on the ants and mosquitoes. "You mustn't worry about malaria," the monk tells me, then proceeds to recount his five-year battle with it in his northern home-monastery, where he almost died several times because of violent fevers.

We talk about the rain, the spicy food, the language. After a while, he leans over and talks to Deh, then speaks to me again in a completely casual voice. "He won't admit it, but I think he's hungry and wants to go home. He was fishing early this morning and I don't imagine he's eaten anything since dawn. Or was it your stomach I heard?"

I look down at my watch and feel hungry myself. We arrived at about ten-thirty and it is now after one. "Maybe it was my stomach. Or was it yours? I'm sorry if we've kept you from lunch."

"I've eaten already. This monastery is very strict in comparison with some I have visited in the south. Here, most of the monks eat only once or twice a day, go to bed at ten and rise at three. But once the body accustoms itself to less sleep, less food, there are no complaints from it, no rumblings.

"I will be going back to the northern monastery in a few days, and probably will not see you again, but do not be lonely for English. Your Thai will come. And do not be lonely for your country and people. The connections you can't see are the deepest, and the Thais will look after you."

After sitting for so long in the feminine Thai position—both legs tucked to one side, a funny kink to the hips—my feet refuse to lift me up. There are pins in my sleeping muscles. The monk, the Ajahn and Deh laugh simultaneously. "That used to happen to me, too," says the monk, "and it gets worse when you start meditating for hours at a time." Within a few minutes, I'm able to bow and rise, and we say goodbye. The Ajahn invites me to come to the monastery whenever I feel that I'm ready.

Once out of the *wat* grounds, Deh kicks in the little bike and we roar off down the road, cutting through the puddles of water, speeding along the edges of the town on the far side of the bridge, where people hang their clothes to dry on fences and trees and eaves. The flowered edges of the narrow roads blur into purple-green ribbons. Near the railway tracks, an old man carrying a load of charcoal on his back hears us coming and raises his hand in greeting. When Deh slows down to pass him, I see his eyes are cataract-swirls of creamy blue.

September 5

WHY A MONK? How can he wear orange and breathe slowly all the time? Sometimes I'm convinced the human race as a whole is pathetic in its stupidity, but I'm beginning to understand why we've survived this long. We have the remarkable ability to get something out of nothing, explanations out of mystery, truth out of air. The great religions and causes are the best magic tricks in history, conjuring neither pigeons nor rabbits. Even an elephant out of a top hat would pale in comparison to the stunning answers we come up with to calm ourselves (or, as the case may be, enrage, justify, avenge ourselves). You don't need to be a Buddhist or a Christian or a Muslim; the truth isn't found only in ancient books. It can be anywhere, depending on your eyes.

If I am to believe the monk, and I do, we mould our lives according to dreams and visions whose substance is purely imagined. Our truths are as numerous and unpredictable as wind currents, as invisible, as undeniable. The only prop necessary for the whole show is faith. With faith, you will have your truth, no matter how absurd it may appear to others. If you have a vision, you're obliged to believe in it even if your neighbours think you're stark raving mad. What must the monk's mother say of her eyebrowless, malnourished son, a perfectly sane young man living on rice and vegetables and pure Asian light? He relinquished his seaside, his clothes, his name, but he knows what he's received in exchange. I like the image of him in my mind, the grey eyes, skin, mouth, the egg-bald head rising out of orange sheets. He is so convinced, so convincing. I wonder about people like him, and the people who are monks without robes, the ones who wander around in the noisier world, their gods in their pockets. Bertrand Russell was once asked if he would die for his beliefs. He laughed and said, "Of course not. After all, I may be wrong." I laugh myself, thinking how wrong I might be. But it doesn't matter. Believe, and the faith feeds itself; truth shines out like a newborn moon.

September 9

I'VE HAD THE SAME DREAM for three nights now. It's a winter dream, beginning with a man walking down a road into the dark. I see him from a height, behind a window; I watch the snow blur cold and silver through the columned light of streetlamps, and the glass of my window is too cold to touch. Or maybe it's too hot—in the dream I know that if I touch it, I'll burn myself. I only stand and watch the man walk away, and he will not turn around to look at me. The soft thud of his feet in the snow is the dream's only sound. It gets louder as the distance between us grows. Somehow

I know that if I push on the window long and hard enough, it will part smoothly under my hands, melt, and I'll be able to get out. But I don't even touch it because of the heat (or coldness). If I pressed my lips to the window for just a moment, the man would come back, but out of fear I don't do it. Instead, I shout his name and wake up.

Michael.

Even when I don't dream I wake at night to turn off the overhead fan. During the days it's sticky and hot; during the nights it's sticky and cool. The breeze from the fan gets under the sheet and shivers me awake. Outside, Denchai sleeps, though a dogfight in the field has torn away a corner of silence. The quiet returns, lies smooth beneath a whirr of insects and frogs. I want to stay awake for this wordlessness. If I cannot have English, let me have this instead. I can understand the silence of sleep, whole in itself, complete.

The days themselves are not whole. They are made of half-eaten words, words left behind, nibbled words too long and strange to get in my mouth or ears. Everything is the wrong size here. My bones are too big, my mind is too small. I never thought words could fail me, but here they're not even words. They're useless noises, wholly unreliable. Meh, Pee-Moi, Koon Yiy, the children all blink innocently at me, smile, shake their heads. It would not matter how very slowly I said, "Please leave me alone in my room for just five minutes." They would not understand. They've lived within fifteen feet of each other for most of their lives. They're afraid to leave me alone.

I write out of tiredness, loneliness, longing. The danger is not that I'll forget anything I left in Canada, but that I'll remember it too sharply. Loneliness is so ironic when I'm surrounded constantly with new people and their lives. The bicycle-rickshaw drivers are anxious to teach me Thai, the children in Nareerat lean over the green terraces and call my Thai names, Kanikaa, Ploy. They're still very shy but sometimes when I'm sitting in the little pavilion under the tamarind tree, they appear quietly, cautious as fawns. If I sing something for them, they will sing the morning assembly songs for me, which I want very much to learn.

It's a terrible thing: to stand in the midst of almost three thousand singing, praying people when you have nothing to sing or pray yourself. I sway in the waves of so much lucent music, but they wash around me instead of through me because I haven't the key, the language, to let them in. The children are teaching me, and they bring roses to the English room, paper bags of sugared fruit and sweet rice. They are very shy, with black-lashed eyes and a velvet cover over their bones. I'm a rare specimen here: the blonde hairs on my arms astound them because my eyebrows are so black. My long Caucasian nose is an absolute mystery. After touching my skin they touch their own, trying to name the differences between us. We understand each other primarily through laughter.

But laughter is too simple a language for me. If I am happy, I am also miserable, prone to emotion, impatience, self-pity. The place and pace of my life have changed so quickly; it's difficult to recognize all this newness as my own life. I've been made into something completely different in less than a month, just because of a long day and night in a plane. In the English room one of the children's storybooks has figures which unfold upwards when the book is opened. (The kids are fascinated by it—Ajahn Champa brought it from England.) I cannot get that image out of my mind, the flat book flipping open, its magical characters rising straight off the page, the scurry of Thai fingers wanting to touch. Thailand itself has opened like that for me, gone from picture books to tangible form, and I am still surprised. The only trick that isn't available is the one that would unfold Canada into three dimensions.

Sometimes I forget this was my choice; I wanted to come here despite what I would leave behind. Apparently (it's on file somewhere) I came here to live and learn in a new culture, to adapt myself to a country very distinct from my own. At the moment, this seems just short of impossible. Even things I know (sunlight on water, fog caught in trees, a long expanse of green) leave me breathless, as though I've never seen colour before. The stars and planets confuse me when I sneak out to the field at night. I turn around and around slowly, testing angles, trying to chalk together a constellation I can recognize. I want an old image. Instead, what I never expected is suddenly there; I see it or am seen by it, caught. Yesterday, I spotted a praying mantis clinging to one of the outer folds of my green curtain, gazing in my direction with the focussed concentration of a tiny silk-green cat.

At night, one sheet sleeps over me and mosquitoes light on my skin. Nothing else, no one, touches me here. After my strange empty dream of snow and hot glass, I don't return easily to sleep. In a place where there is nothing for you, no prayers or songs or even stars, you turn blindly to your body, hug your shoulders in the dark and touch your own pale arms, amazed. This is how I know I'm alone. My own skin surprises me.

September 15

TONIGHT IT RAINS so hard the tin roof of the badminton court might splinter and spray us with shrapnel. We have to shout to hear each other. We've been playing since six, and all of Denchai has had a good laugh at the *falang* competing with and losing to kids who are half her size. *Hahahaha*, all night long. The quickness of the game is exhausting. The Thais, who play from the time they can hold a racquet, have me at a disadvantage. The children wonder out loud if there is something wrong with my arms. Lin is growing bored with tapping the birdie back and forth with me. She keeps glancing at the open door.

"Kalen! Do you want wing?" *Wing?* There is a brief conference to determine the meaning of the word in English, followed by a triumphant shout, "Lun!"

"Ah, run."

"Yes, yes, lun, lun!"

So we quit the muggy air of the court without another word and lun into the great wash of storm. Within two minutes our pace slackens because of the weight of water in our clothes and shoes. We stumble through the puddles, laughing. There is a delicious wickedness in doing something so unexpected, so un-Thai. Once over the bridge, we stop playing and really begin to work. We splash past the shuttered stores, the barbershop, the crumbling old cinema, the police station, past a hundred people and their two hundred eyes glittering out from under the eaves. At the edge of the town we turn around and run back only because Lin is afraid to go farther.

We return to the court breathless and drenched. We burst in the door like two wet dogs, covered with mud and howling with glee about how terrible we are. Only after we've leaned over to shake out our hair do we notice Prasit sitting patiently in a wicker chair with his arms folded. Obviously, he's been wondering if I'm still alive. "Sawatdee-ka," I say, and *wai* deeply, the Thai bow of head to hands. For a long moment he simply looks at me, which immediately makes me conscious of the hair plastered to my forehead and cheeks, my soaked shirt. He directs a nasty glare to Lin, who quickly transforms into a weak creature with vulnerable wrists. Her face changes in Prasit's presence; her eyes lower. She is no longer the girl who could kill someone with a badminton racquet. Instead, she seems to be on the verge of tears. Prasit ushers us both out of the court, leaving all the players (Deh, Boh, Sak, Joum, Sulin) staring after us. All this quiet stern drama, I'm thinking, as if we've been vandalizing Buddhas. He begins to fuss and cackle. "You not want to get sick, do you? You must go quick and take bath and get dry or you will be sick. Quick, quick." We have reached Lin's house by this time and she talks softly to Prasit, *wai*s very slowly and winks at me. (I have already taught her the wholly *falang* habit of winking.) "Bye-bye," she chirps, slipping into her family's shop.

Prasit explains to me how cold the rain is, how terribly ill I could get. I say, "But Paw Prasit, I am Canadian. I come from a cold country."

"Yes, yes, of course." He nods vigorously. "You are Canadian. We must look after you. If any bad things happen, we will be in trouble with Canada. You are like one of our children."

The other day, Ajahn Champa said, "Sometimes the best answer is to smile and nod." I smile and nod. Being like one of "their" children means I have almost two dozen Thai fathers. A sobering thought. When we arrive at the liquor store, Prasit chatters with Pee-Moi and I am sent up to bathe. "Goodnight, Miss Kalen," he calls as I go up the stairs, dripping rain and mud. "Please take care."

Smile and nod. "Ka," I reply, the polite, feminine all-purpose word. "Ka, Paw Prasit. Goodnight." In the *hongnam*, I pour cold water over myself, shivering now, wishing for a water heater. I'm weak from badminton and running, barely able to get the cap off the shampoo bottle; my fingerbones have softened to rubber. I finish bathing, wrap myself in a towel and run dripping up the staircase to my room.

It's still storming outside. The entire top floor is flashing blue and silver and black shadows. I dry myself off in the dark, shivers licking up my back and down my legs with such force that I brush them away with the towel, imagining ants, lizards. The cast-iron spirals barring the outside of the windows fall in shadows on the floor, scrawling a strange calligraphy, very much like the Thai letters I'm learning to write, all hooks and coils. I step into those dark lines and look down at the words on my skin, a script I understand because it touches me.

And tonight, a new dream. Strangers standing in a deep blue-grey field beneath a dark sky. They are restless and quick-eyed. From a great distance I see them standing together in long whipping grass, looking to the sky and dreading the storm. They cringe, cower at the bursts of noise above them, staring upwards with unhinged jaws, amazed by the first lightning they have ever known.

September 21

IT'S RAINED SO MUCH that frogs and toads are drowning. At least one took refuge indoors last night. This morning, unable to push my foot into my shoe, I shook a toad from my vile Mary Janes. He hopped groggily across the cement until Pee-Moi scooped him up and tossed him into the rose garden. The sky is inexhaustible and takes up new storms daily. Rivers that didn't exist last week run in the ravines and paths between houses. I expect to see live fish slap down the gutters.

When we walk to the market to catch a *songtow* for school, Lin and the other girls complain about the weather, huddling up two by two under umbrellas. I've never seen such brilliant umbrellas. It's as though the heavy rains have caused an epidemic growth of exotic mushrooms. At the market entrance, a few *songtow*s are waiting for passengers and we crawl into the one which seems to offer the best shelter. These little trucks are used in lieu of buses to transport commuters to and from Prae, the provincial capital, and other nearby villages. I'm used to them now but only because I put all thoughts of a violent death out of mind on the third trip. Now I just try to enjoy the scenery. We sit in two long rows in the back, under a metal frame covered by canvas or plastic or thin aluminum sheets, and usually five children sit on little wooden stools in the narrow middle space, crammed between our knees. Often there are market women going to Prae with their chickens and fish, or farmers who bring along a couple of hoes and one of their old-fashioned rifles. There is never much room. The driver tries to squeeze in as many fares as he can each trip, even if it means nearly asphyxiating us in the process. Three or four boys often hang, wind-battered, at the back of the truck. They won't let girls do this.

It isn't exactly comfortable, but it's always interesting. No pillow-faced bus-riders here, politely trying not to touch anyone's knees. In a *songtow*, we practically sit on each other. The drivers are very different, too. Thai drivers don't really believe in other vehicles. They think their *songtow* is the only one in the world, and they swerve into the oncoming lane of traffic to pass herds of bicycles or goats whenever they so desire. It doesn't matter if other cars are coming straight for us—the driver thinks he's seeing a mirage. We pass the other people in the oncoming truck closely enough to see their teeth, but the driver doesn't notice. He just careens along, brown elbow sticking out the window, radio turned up full blast.

Generally, the tires are bald, but this hardly makes a difference if the driver never plans to use his brakes. They think it's always better to accelerate. The first couple of times I rode in a *songtow*, I imagined accidents: metal bars stuck in my spine, smoking wrecks, my end coming for me at ninety-five miles per hour in the form of a lumbering elephant. Elephants regularly appear on the roads with people sitting on their necks like oversized cowbirds. It would be a ludicrous way to die, I think, here, on the edge of rice paddies, in a little Tonka truck driven by a singing lunatic.

Of course, I can't die. I am loved. Someone in Canada is waiting for me. We've planned long, perfect lives together. Untimely death is not part of the story. The hassle alone of getting my body home would drive my family crazy.

This morning, in the *songtow* speeding towards Nareerat, all the girls weave their arms together and sit curved over, teeth chattering. They say the wind is made of ice, but I don't find it too cold. The twenty kilometres of fields between Denchai and Prae have disappeared behind a blown curtain of fog. Rain sprays into the truck and our shirts stick to our backs. The clouds outside are very low. If I walked across one of the fields, I would emerge on the other side with shreds of cloud caught in my hair.

IT STOPPED RAINING for a while at noon, pretended to clear, but turned again at two. The sky is iron blue, darkened to charcoal over the centre of Prae, and a wolfish wind leaps in all the open windows of the school, tearing exam sheets off desks and flinging entire magazines to the floor. Thunder growls above us now; everyone keeps pausing at her work to look out the nearest window. I have watched Ajahn Champa do this several times, become still and tense while gazing out over the pale green schoolhouses of Nareerat. If she twitched her nose and sniffed the air, I would believe in reincarnation; she might have been a gazelle in her last life. When Ajahn Yupa and Ajahn Sangkaya gave me my Thai lessons today, neither they nor I could concentrate for more than five minutes at a time. This wind blew into our ears and swept out our brains. Ajahn Yupa didn't want to do anything but giggle with me about Canadian men while Sangkaya and I discussed in detail the miracle of contact lenses. The children are the most restless, galloping down the hallways, then sliding into class in their stocking feet. Our identical black shoes sit in rows outside the rooms, sleeping beetles under the upturned umbrellas. No one thinks to close the umbrellas until the wind starts hurling them into the assembly field, rousing shouts from the second and third floor. Children rush down the stairs and race after the flying mushrooms.

Finally, after brooding all afternoon long, the storm breaks and roars, shuddering great, intermittent blazes over Prae, gleaming on the gold minarets of the temple, tinting the fretwork glass a strange purplish grey. The monks scurry onto the monastery terraces like orange ants; they pull down their drying robes and bolt the windows. Holding armfuls of saffron laundry, they turn faces up to the eaves where the temple bells swing and clang against the rain gutters. Lightning shoots in long veins across the sky, emptying only to fill up again, and the children scream, "I saw your bones, I saw your bones!" every time the light cracks down.

The power goes out when the rain crashes in, completing the loss of concentration. Children laugh and whinny and stamp around like wild ponies. Ajahn Champa sighs at her desk. She keeps saying how terrible the teachers are these days, they can't even control their students, they don't know their jobs. She is terribly serious. I want to say, "Ajahn, the storm makes them behave like this," just as one would say, "Father, it's the Devil. . . ." I say nothing, though, only shake my head in silent commiseration and busy myself by closing the shutters.

Within ten minutes messengers are sent around to the separate teaching halls. Students may be dismissed for the day. Study is impossible in lightless, shuttered rooms with herds of ponies. Lin comes to the English room with other girls from Denchai. They try to shout above each other and the snarl of thunder.

Who has an umbrella? I've lost my shoe! But it's right there! No, that's the *falang*'s. Is it behind the door? Where did you last take it off? Aah, here, under the stairs. Do you have an umbrella or not? What? Then we can't walk through Prae, we'll get wet. Run? The *falang* likes to run. But the rain. *Falangs* are always rushing around, they love running, never go slow. *Jai yen yen.* Lin? Lin! *Bai nai?*

We are off again, across the assembly field, out the high open gates of Nareerat, past the monastery and into the twisted streets of Prae. We leap over the puddles and trip on the chipped curbs, our shoes squelching water. Lin takes complicated short cuts between buildings and through temple yards, but we are still soaked when we get to the *songtow* stop where Deh and Sak wait for us. The little girl Joum, who lives with Lin's family, is with them, too, pulling a wet sweater around her shoulders. We crawl into an empty *songtow* and the driver screeches onto the road.

The rain is cooler than it was this morning. Joum snuggles up against me. It gets even colder and darker when we enter the teak grove midway between Prae and Denchai.

Suddenly—but much faster than that—we are all tossed into each other, a mix of bones banging in a can, Sak's elbows in my ribs, Joum's small body knocked clear into and over mine, against the cab of the truck, Deh's skull caught up under his sister's chin. In one jerking breath we skid to a stop.

Stillness. Silence.

We pull away from each other. Joum's eyes have taken over her whole face. She should probably be crying from being tossed up against the truck, but she is too surprised. We gather our senses. The crashing rain returns to us. We smell cold mist, crushed green, gasoline. We look at each other, shaken and shaking, then hear the driver curse and slam his door.

Deh is the first to make a noise. He throws back his head, laughs and says, "Naa Pee-Kalen shee cao muuc!" which I understand perfectly despite my elementary Thai. It means, "The face of older sister Karen is very white." Everyone laughs at this but my sense of humour just isn't Thai enough yet. Sak's elbow has made a fair dent in my side. I am just starting to get my breath again.

Deh hops out of the truck to see what's happened. A massive old teak tree is downed in front of us, its trunk almost as thick as the truck is high. It stretches far across the road and hundreds of its branches are splintered open. Teak flowers are scattered everywhere, and foot-wide teak leaves are plastered to the windshield, the roof of the *songtow*, the road.

I don't ask. Why ask? Smile, nod, don't ask. Besides, the driver wouldn't understand my Thai. When did that tree fall? If it was down before we entered the woods, why didn't the driver slow down sooner? If it fell just now, just by blind chance, why didn't we hear it crash? Could we have mistaken the crash for thunder? Do big trees blow over just like that in this country? That's impossible. Perhaps it was struck by lightning. That would have been worth seeing. It probably happened this afternoon, when the storm started up again. The driver misjudged the distance when he saw the tree; that's why we skidded to a stop.

The truck lurches far off the road to pass the fallen tree. I push against the roof of the *songtow*, steadying myself; the rain strikes against the canvas like a madman thumping on a drum. We slide and spin back onto the road, begin to fly over the sleek blackness again, speeding to get out of the trees. The ground beneath us is sprayed green with broken plants.

September 22

SPEAKING OF STORMS: the body has its own.

I will have to go to a doctor, I suppose, a thought which I find abhorrent. Thai modesty and shame have already rubbed off on me, but this is ridiculous. Menstrual cycles are not supposed to last twenty-six days. Why is my body doing this to me? How can it be so inconsiderate? After the hell of chili peppers and spices, why this? This whole Thai adventure was a foolish idea. No brave fronts. I am miserable today. Sadness knits itself together here; I'm never sad about one thing in particular but a long chain of things—I get so melodramatic. I've spent hours these last two days in the Prae post office, trying to call Canada. We couldn't get a connection because of all the storms. When the phone finally did ring today, that is *all* it did. I called in the morning, afternoon, evening, just to listen to a telephone shrilling in my ear. There I sat in the air-conditioned communications room, freezing, while the male operators politely ignored me. A few times, they each gave me long, velvet-brown looks of sympathy, identical to the sympathy of cocker spaniels; this made me want to sob. I wrote "Pleasepleaseplease" on a little slip of paper beside the telephone, but begging long distance does not work.

It is idiotic to love someone so far away with such desperation. I sleep with his letters. I write small novels to him every day, describing my life's most intricate details. I see him in everything, walk around whispering "I love you"

33

to the inanimate objects I know he has touched, certain pieces of clothing, certain books. I think my skin is too thin to hold all this in, that man, that country, this one. I will crack open and spill, or dissolve, melt away in this hot valley.

When I went back to the post office in the afternoon, then at six, the two spaniel-eyed operators were waiting for me with a glass of Chinese tea and a new sheet of paper for my petitions to the god of long distance. When the first rings started (the silence in the room was such that the men could hear the line), they looked both pained and hopeful. When no one answered and salt water began dripping off my chin onto the lap of my school uniform, they tactfully turned away and played with their machines, allowing me to sit for a moment.

One of them produced a clean white handkerchief. (I always manage to be without them when I need them.) The other said, "Jai yen yen." Cool your heart. I am beginning to love the Thais. They are gentle.

October 1, 1986

AFTER BADMINTON and a bath, the evening slows down. I watch cartoons with Noi and Geway or I help Koon Yiy sew patches on an old quilt which acquires new holes even as we mend the old ones. I often go for a walk with Lin and Deh along Yantrak, stopping to talk to Joum, Boh or Sak along the way. I'm finally starting to remember names now, though usually I say them with the wrong tone.

Tonight we wander up the street while Lin says the alphabet, pausing so I can repeat each letter. It takes a while to get through some seventy letters. All the consonants come first, then about thirty vowels. The vowels make us sound like strange hooting animals. Deh runs ahead, laughing. When we're in the middle of the bridge, he leans over the rail, his eyes and mouth wide open. The river slips under us in darkness. We see nothing below but the white *chong-nang* flowers on the far bank. Deh whispers, "Glua pee mai?" Afraid of what? I turn to Lin, who explains *pee* means ghost. Am I afraid of ghosts? "What ghosts?"

Deh stares at me for a moment, then frowns. "The ghosts who live under the bridge. They can kill you. You can't go down to the river at night." I question Lin with a glance and see that she, too, believes this. "Ghosts live in all dark places in Denchai." She contemplates the well of shadow before us and adds, "And in Prae." An exhaled breath. "And in all the north."

Deh finishes with a solemn whisper, "In all meu-ung thai, everywhere."

They tell me to be careful. There are ghosts under the bridge, in corners, under fallen trees, in the abandoned railway shed. They are afoot and very much alive.

We leave the menace beneath the bridge. Lin suggests we go to watch a tennis match. We walk towards the railroad station. I didn't know a tennis court existed in Denchai. Tennis is disdained by the badminton group. It is too cumbersome, with that racquet heavy as a frying pan. Badminton is light and quick, better suited to Asian bones. "Tennis is beu-uh," Lin says. Boring.

"There are ghosts there, too, and many tennis balls," says Deh.

"Where?"

"Over there," she points to the far side of the court. Beyond the high fence is a deep ravine. If a ball flies out into that darkness, it is lost forever. The Professor, as everyone calls the tennis coach, has offered the children money to go down into the ravine and find the balls, but the offer isn't generous enough to combat their fear of ghouls and thorny plants and snakes. No one will search for the balls, even in daylight. They grow moss.

Lin takes me to the court and introduces me to The Professor, a good-looking man who almost speaks English. He wants to teach me tennis on a regular basis. "Good arms," he says, eyeing my biceps. The tennis court is full of good arms; I notice in particular a tall, slim woman who seems to be beating her male opponent. Even more remarkably, she is wearing shorts.

After she finishes her match, I meet Beed and her

husband on the bleachers inside the tennis compound. She's the first Thai woman I've ever met with a loud voice. Her husband's name is Samat. He's also very tall for a Thai, and has a curly black goatee that makes him look like a legendary Burmese giant. Their daughter Poun sits on his knee eating a cookie; she is painted with chocolate. Though Beed speaks English, she refuses to use it very much and prefers Thai. "In two months, you will speak Thai better than I speak English, yes, and you will laugh at me, yes, yes, I know." I protest, complain about the tones, which I'll never be able to learn. She laughs. "English and its many verb tenses are much worse than a few notes of music." We practise the rising and falling sounds while a doubles match is played; she makes a face when I say them wrong. If the tones are off, the meaning of the words can be lost completely, or confused with other words, sometimes the most embarrassing words possible.

"You come to our house and I show you my birds," Beed says. "I show you my father's garden." She lives near the outskirts of Denchai where her family runs the service station.

Lin and Deh are clearly bored with watching tennis balls fly back and forth under the harsh lights of the court. Deh is playing with a large beetle on the end of a stick. Lin nudges me, "I take you to Beed's house tomorrow. Now we go for nampun." *Nampun* is a drink made from crushed ice and blended fruit, sold on the street by a regular vendor; a glass of *nampun* is equivalent to a trip for ice-cream. I shout goodbye to Beed, who is already on the court again, bounding from one side to another, smacking back fast low shots. As we leave, Samat says his wife is just lucky.

(HERE BEGAN MY FRIENDSHIP with Beed and her entire family. She, Samat and her parents were four of the most tolerant, helpful people I knew in Denchai. Every small town has its attitudes, superstitions, gossips, but Beed and her family, though the epitome of "Thai-ness," never had small-town prejudices. They were remarkably broad-minded, often very wise, and gave me great moral support, especially during the first six months of my stay, when being Thai in a foreigner's body was most difficult.)

October 5

I CAN NO LONGER IGNORE REALITY. It has been more than a month. I must remember that a pelvic examination never killed anyone, even in Asia. (And yet—how can I be sure?) I've told Ajahn about the problem and, distressed as she is, she's even managed to give me a choice between doctors: a female who speaks no English and a male who speaks some. I surprise her by choosing the one of the opposite sex. I am anxious for English. If I'm dying, I don't want to hear about it through a translator.

Ajahn Yupa takes me to the old wooden building of the clinic, not far from Nareerat, tucked away in a grove of teak and banana trees. The long terrace is strewn with people dozing in the afternoon heat. Loose-skinned old men and women perch on stools, regularly wiping their faces and necks with handkerchiefs. After we pull up on Yupa's scooter, the general glances in our direction lengthen into stares.

Yupa ushers me into the small office, shows me to the nurses, sits me down and rushes off to her next class. The other Thais watch her run down the steps, then, in a perfectly orchestrated swivel of necks, turn and gaze at me. I wait for a long time, knees chastely closed and sweating under the heavy blue skirt. I'd like to shake it out over my legs, but I've been told that's too unladylike. The nurses are giggly. We run through all the Thai questions I know, the ones I've been asked about six hundred times already and therefore can manage without problems. It's dangerous to know how to speak a little because they get carried away, and talk on and on while I am completely lost in the music of the language, understanding nothing but their eyes. I can handle the regulars: what is your name, how old are you, where are you from, are you happy today, is Thailand beautiful, is the food good or too hot, do you like Thai boys, do you have a Thai boyfriend, do you want one? I want to be able to say, "Do you have one for sale?" but I'm not sure if they would see the humour in this. Sarcasm is often lost on the Thais. I've tried to be sarcastic to Ajahn Champa, but often she takes me seriously or just looks at me in a curious way.

I'm suspicious of these nurses. They look younger than me; they aren't wearing little white hats. In fact, the whole place is sorely lacking that sterilized, scrubbed look I find both repellent and comforting in hospitals. It may be cold and clinical, but at least it's clean. Here, for example, they don't pull a white sheet down over the wooden examining table. You sit among germs. Bony old people hobble in one after another, wriggle up and peg down on their elbows, then lean over to receive a large needle in the rump. This takes place right in the office, while the nurses ask me over their shoulders if I want to marry a Thai man and live here forever. I'm beginning to worry they'll examine me in public, too. The old people often look right at me and even smile in their embarrassment. I quickly return their smiles and look away.

Above the table rise shelves stacked with a flowery assortment of pills in ten-gallon jars. Syringes lie in rows below the pills. The nurses seem to give every patient a handful of the same pills in a little plastic bag and an injection in the behind. Is there an epidemic rampaging through the countryside?

Finally the doctor appears, a cheerful penguin of a man who immediately asks, "What the problem?" I begin to explain. Like many doctors, he nods as if he already knew the problem and was asking just to be polite. After speaking to the nurses, he waddles off down the hall. The nurse smiles apologetically and motions me to follow her. We enter another room; she mimes instructions and leaves me. I stand alone in the room looking out the window, where a group of *sam-lah* drivers watches me with interest. I struggle with the blinds until they drop with a clatter. The nurse returns and leaves a bundle of rags on the examining table, which unfortunately has begun to remind me of a very large cutting board. Mortified, I slide off my skirt and underwear, and sit on the cool wood.

The nurse enters and unwraps the rags, revealing a shiny metal object which looks like one of those kitchen gadgets for crushing garlic. The room darkened when I closed the blinds; I can't make out the gleaming instrument until the doctor comes in and picks it up. I'm told to lie back and relax. I realize the strange piece of silver is a speculum, an antique, wrapped up in dust-cloths, unused, taken out once a year to be polished like a trophy. I cannot help myself. Before he begins the examination, I ask, "Is that clean? Are you sure? How clean is that?" He laughs and assures me everything is completely sanitary. The rags, I suppose, are simply stained. Is it possible for stained things to be sterile?

During the exam, the nurse holds a camping flashlight over the doctor's head so he can see what he's doing. What is he doing? I slowly realize that, despite my clenched stomach muscles, this is one of the events I will laugh about later. This is a "wonderful experience." On the ceiling I make out a large spider, thin-legged with an impressively bulbous thorax. All through the exam I stare at it, wondering if the pressure of my eyes will make it fall off the ceiling.

When the doctor finishes, he tells me, "You fine. You got little infection, little problem. Not enough iron. Not serious. We give you some antibiotic, some vitamin, and you be better in a week." He talks hurriedly to the nurse, washes his hands and shuffles away before I can even ask him exactly what is wrong with me. The nurse delicately turns her head while I put on my clothes, then takes me back to the office. I get an injection. The other nurse sees me and laughs with delight. "Sabai dee mai ka?" Yes, I tell her, I am fine. She prepares two little bags of pills for me and I pay a small amount of money for the drugs. "Choke-dee, na-ka," she says, wishing me luck. I step out onto the porch, into the warmth of curious eyes and gold air. The trees are lit from a good angle now, leaves glowing the rare green of caught sunlight. I clutch my little bags of pills and walk through the rusty gates of the clinic, already feeling healed.

October 14

THESE ARE THE PHOTOGRAPHS I don't take, can't take, scenes without explanations because I have none. Images materialize once or every day and seem impossible to catch except with my own eyes. Even writing them is nothing, not nearly enough, not real. With words I never quite touch the bones. Living here makes me want to paint, to get at the colour and form of what I see. I don't even understand half of it. Sometimes I don't know the words for the questions I want to ask. I'll have to stay here forever to learn all I need to know.

Boum, a girl from Nareerat who also lives in Denchai, walks with me through Prae. We are on our way to the square where the *songtow*s wait when a mammoth blue truck screeches around the corner. Men from the fields are piled in the back and hanging off the edges, gripping the roof, and every one of them howls or pounds on a drum or tambourine. Even after the truck roars down the main street and disappears, I still hear music ringing off the monastery walls. Boum looks back at me—my mouth is open. She hasn't even stopped walking, whereas I'm staring after the truck in awe. "Mai pen lai," she says, "never mind," and pulls on my arm. What were the men singing? Why?

One morning, in a rush to buy pineapple for Meh without missing my *songtow*, I almost walk over a little gnome seated in the midst of the morning throng. He has the thin face and scraggled beard of a goat. Breathing serenely into a bamboo flute, he occasionally closes his dirty gold eyes as though he's put himself to sleep. Two tin cups sit in front of each knee, but I have no time to give him money; the crowd carries me towards the fruit stalls. When I look back, he's hidden in a thicket of legs.

On random mornings a dozen black-haired girls meet under the tamarind trees to juggle limes before class. With the skill of accomplished clowns, they sing and dance as they juggle, dismayed to hear that most Canadians never learn this art. They play until the first bell rings, which invariably makes them screech in unison, drop the limes and rush to their prospective school buildings. When they press their hands over their mouths to stifle their giggling, I imagine the lime scent they smell. Then they are gone, and I am once again late for my Thai lesson.

In the rose garden at home, we have a beautiful, leather-coloured lizard striped chocolate brown, his head like the long sloped skull of a snake. He is a fat lizard accustomed to the luxury of enormous and frequent meals. The butterflies here have wingspans as wide as my hands; the dragonflies are so heavy they seem to fly slower than Canadian dragonflies. Everything is oversized and must be easier to catch for the reptiles. (This is probably untrue, but it sounds good.) Hooked like fishing nets between the telephone lines, spider webs twitch trapped insects. Purple-headed birds torpedo through the air with whips of grass hanging from their beaks. I greet these strange lives with surprise, and feel like whispering *thank you* every time I blink. So much is alive, so much sings, crawls, clambers. I'm shouted at by the world itself. Sometimes I open my eyes in the morning and the praying mantis sits on the green quilt a few inches from my head, washing her face and forelegs.

42

The Thais don't understand my fascination, the way I hang like a dog out the *songtow* windows and stare. There is no lens wide enough to catch a single field here, no lens but an eye's, a mind's hungry scope. The flooded fields offer a precise reflection of the sky, where clouds spill and build themselves up for miles. When the sun reaches her low, blinding angle, the wet rice paddies shine silver, but in the falling dusk or the mist at dawn, they are shadowed, cross-hatched like the backs of splendid turtles. Forests rise on the hills beyond Denchai, woven in clouds, threading my mind with stories of children lost in imaginary lands. Often the Thais don't perceive their world as I do, because they've seen it all their lives and love it thoughtlessly. I continue to be awed every morning on the careening journey to Prae.

October 20

THE MORNING OPENS cool and clouded, giving me a sky of ash rose, scarlet, then clear gold shafting down into the hills. With practise, I see more and more every day. Seeing grace is easy here because the people are born into it. Even women walking to work in the fields move with the clean-curved backs of dancers.

The natural grace of the Thai makes my dancing class pure hell. Imagine a gorilla doing ballet. Imagine an enormous white chicken in red diapers. This is Karen learning classical Thai dance. I am with the youngest, smallest girls in Nareerat, the beginners. Beside them, I am monstrous. We wear baggy red wrap-pants (they really do look like longish diapers) and the string on my pants always gets knotted by the end of the hour class. One of the little girls usually has to bite it off for me.

Fawn-ram thai is an exercise in intricacy and patience. Unlike in jazz or gymnastics, it's impossible to overlook or conceal small flaws in the speed and flash of the movements themselves. In fawn-ram thai there is no flash. You move slowly, in perfect time with the music, which often sounds to me like cats making love during a concerto of untuned violas and piccolos. (My own fault; my appreciation of ethnic music is not up to par.)

Fawn-ram thai is an exercise in frustration. I never felt uncoordinated until I started it. I sweat profusely from mere concentration, because one hardly moves at all. To manage the one-leg balances and arched fingers and shifts of hands all at the same slow time requires an unprecedented amount of thought, and personally I would rather go jogging, but that's not very cultural. I would love to try *moo-aye thai*—Thai boxing, the martial art of the country—but Ajahn Champa won't hear of such a thing. "I refuse to be responsible for broken ribs," she said, rubbing her forehead with the heel of her hand in a gesture of despair.

So I learn dancing instead, and it's the closest I've ever come to ritualized worship. *Fawn-ram thai* is not so much dance for me as it is ceremony. Sometimes, when a small miracle allows me to move all my parts in time, bow my head, kneel, join my hands in the classical *wai*, I haven't accomplished a routine, a dance, at all. I've said a wordless prayer.

November 1, 1986

LATE TONIGHT, I had two surprises, miracles actually. One: the telephone in the liquor store worked. Two: I talked to Michael.

He is not dead. He is not even dying, or violently ill. The only reason there was never an answer in the apartment is because he was never home. I've already written a long letter to him; the overhead fan has blown the first four pages behind the desk where the ants are devouring a large dead moth. I have cried for a few hours already, dehydrating myself. All very miserable and melodramatic, but that's what's called for. He isn't just seeing another woman, he isn't even just sleeping with another woman.

He's moved in with her.

He spoke of his pain, his suffering, the difficulty of living alone, surrounded by "ghosts of the past."

Ghosts! Thailand is literally crawling with them. What's so terrible about ghosts of the past—they are more trustworthy than Thai ghosts. He says writing letters isn't enough. Fine, but couldn't he just have an affair? Why does he have to live with her? Here I am, among all the curious, staring, eternally laughing Thais, without real toilets or washing machines or English or peanut butter or a single human being who really knows me, and Michael whines long distance about loneliness and love.

He says she makes wonderful suppers. Beautiful. I eat my fish guts every week with a grin; I pick voracious ants out of my underwear each morning, praying all the while that our dear Michael is well.

What a fool.

Suddenly, I feel the world physically, feel the chasm of distance. Even in the sea there are entire mountain ranges and deserts. How far away, exactly, am I? The earth isn't a globe, as in school, but a knuckled fist, a labyrinth of bone and stone, the deep places flooded and unfathomable. The dark of Denchai sweeps up around me; even the dogs are silent. I feel ugly, untouchable, like a creature whose function is mysterious or repellent: a slug, a leech, some microscopic bug. I want to slip into the fields and sleep in grass and mud, let my breath take up the rhythm of the earth's. I *feel* memories glide through me like sharp-finned fish; they turn twice, shift to shadow; light slides off their scales and they disappear.

He said, "I can't split myself down the middle for you." He needs my physical presence, my body. He wants me to come home. But it's too late for that now. He said he still loves me, still wants me to write, still . . .

I fall asleep crying.

November 5

LAST NIGHT IN THE HONGNAM, a lizard fell off the wall into the water basin as I reached in with a bucket. He swam with his legs pulled back, nosing against the tiles, unable to get any kind of grip. I lifted him up, surprised to touch the rice-paper skin. I could see his heart thumping at my hand.

His claws were small enough to feel soft, and the black wax-drop eyes stared without blinking. His heart was there on my hand—a shiver went up my wet arm. I might have grown a few scales if I'd held him longer.

Once, in Africa, Isak Dinesen received devastating news. She went outside to look for a sign, something to tell her how to proceed. She watched a rooster rip a lizard's tongue out of its mouth. Then she had to pound the twitching reptile to death with a stone. I was luckier. I nudged the lizard onto the cold floor. He rested motionless for a moment, then sprang onto the wall and up. I went to sleep with his life still pulsing in my hand.

November 6

BEED SAVES ME from feeling sorry for myself. Dear Beed with her indomitable backhand and Western shorts. I walk slowly up Yantrak (I've been walking slowly for several days now), wanting only to speak to someone who will understand me, who will listen. I reach the gas station, but Beed is not alone. The entire family is out in front, having an argument about geraniums. They're trying to beautify the station, and Beed's mother wants geraniums instead of roses. "There are enough roses already. Geraniums are rare. They will have to come from Chiang Mai."

Everyone hushes to a whisper when I appear: it's all over Denchai that the *falang* has been somewhat hysterical these last few days, has even been crying in public. Paw Prasit comes to see me every day to make sure I'm not dying.

Beed's father smiles and asks if I've been swimming; my eyes are so red. I'm not sure if this is a joke or not. I begin an attempt at calm explanation but it quickly turns into English and Thai gibberish verging on tears. For a moment, Beed, her husband and her parents are silent. Little Poun, who did not notice me until I began to sputter, also begins to cry, which fortunately takes everyone's attention away from me. I blow my nose. (Finally I am remembering handkerchiefs.)

A truck has pulled up to the pumps and before going to fill it, Samat makes a strange clicking noise with his teeth and says, "Kalen, kohn soo-wai, mai pen lai." Beautiful one, never mind. I laugh in spite of myself; the last thing I am now is beautiful. Beed takes me by the hand and leads me to the office, with still-snivelling Poun perched on her hip. Her parents follow close behind. Once inside the sunny office, Koon Meh takes down the Chinese checkerboard. The little grease-monkey named Chet comes in to play with me.

"There are a thousand good men in Canada," Beed tells me.

"And many millions of great Thai men right here," says her father.

"You should find a new Thai boyfriend who is not rai-jai," Beed's mother says. *Rai-jai* means many-hearted, without one true heart. "We all love the people who are closest to us. You are very far away. But don't worry. You are young and will be close to many."

"You should marry my brother," chirps Chet, who is quite small, even for a Thai. "He's a policeman who will take good care of you."

Out of eight matches of Chinese checkers, I win only twice, when Beed's mother plays. She lets me win. I don't care. I'm not even angry that they don't take all this very seriously. Samat says "Mai pen lai" every time my face begins to crumble. "Don't think," advises Beed's father. "First it will give you headache, then it will make you old." I play checkers until I am half blind, then, without thinking, I walk home through the green-gold light of dusk. After my chicken and rice and a discussion with Pee-Moi about duck eggs, I go to bed, sleeping deeply for the first time in weeks, without a memory of dreams.

November 9

WE ARE SOMEWHERE outside the city of Piegit. After following
a narrow, jungle-choked road, we arrived in Paw Prasert's
village, the house where he was born, the streets he grew up
in and was lucky enough to leave. He has ten brothers and
sisters who also have left the village, and just his parents live
here now. (They live part-time in Denchai, too—staying two
weeks there, two weeks here.)

Prasert's siblings have also arrived, and the family becomes
a great, serpentine creature sliding and whispering and roaring with laughter on all three floors of the house, in both
Chinese and Thai. Thai seems so much smoother than Chinese,
but perhaps that's simply because I understand it. Chinese is
a mystery, though it sounds familiar because it's also tonal.
Prasert's younger brother teaches me to count to ten in Chinese and feeds me Mandarin oranges all afternoon long, asking
questions with such enthusiasm that I don't get bored. Sometimes it's difficult to spend hours and hours with Thai people
because they talk so much about food, the weather, mosquitoes. The rest of the world, and whatever might be happening
in it, is rarely a concern; I don't even know what's going on
anymore. After spending the entire afternoon eating fruit
and Chinese pastries, and drinking black iced coffee by the
jug, Prasert says, "I'm hungry." We troop into the street.

The road is so narrow I can hear people sneeze across the
way. I can see the hands of clocks inside the other houses.
Every dwelling-place is connected, wooden, two or three
storeys high, crowded with children, young women,
grandmothers and grandfathers perched on wicker chairs
and wooden benches. Their lives wrap around me; I trip
again and again over the tails of Chinese words. It's as though
I've changed countries or am dreaming of China. To see all
the people is only the first picture: beneath the surface are
the stories, the events, all the ways lives swing out on their
own. Being immersed suddenly in this village makes me

remember how far I am from knowing anything. People stare at me openly—*falangs* never appear here. Women come over from the noodle-stands to get a good look. When we enter the market-place, the fruit and vegetable sellers meet my eyes; Pee-Moi clutches my arm and nods at everyone. She is proud of me, the rarity. In Denchai and Prae, I am no longer so special, but here, I'm once again completely strange.

Suddenly, there is a great crash not far away from us, followed by a yelp and the shouts of children and men. A man carrying metal chairs has tripped over a yellow dog and crashed to the ground. No one seems hurt but the cowering mongrel, who whisks under a stage set-up and whines.

Pee-Moi tells me the stage is for a Chinese opera, which explains the festive air of the market. Even as we speak, the stage is being set in a red and gold shimmer. Prasert says the singers and acrobats will perform as long as they can, with the best of them still onstage at daybreak.

The market is a performance in itself. I want to keep the expression on one of the children's faces, or record one moment of sound, or capture the smell of the roasting blue corn. Watermelons open like giant flowers; oysters, lobsters, sausages and chickens rise upwards in pyramids; Thailand's exotic shelled and spiny fruits grow like sea anemones out of crates and carts. People carry expensive oranges, apples and Chinese cakes on silver platters, taking the food to the temple. The scent of incense mixes with the smell of fried chicken and roasted bananas.

By the time the opera begins, we've eaten so much we can't get up. We sit at our table instead of being pressed close in with the sweaty crowd. Music whips up as suddenly as the wind, and the combination of the two tickles the people: they're laughing, throwing firecrackers and jumping up and down. The scarlet canopy over us ripples and shakes. When the singers begin, I am stunned by the high-pitched toiling of so many tongues. The acrobats appear soon after the singers; they toss themselves in the air without a thought to gravity.

The music is incomprehensible to me and may give me nightmares, but the spectacle itself is glorious. The costumes are more elaborate than any I've ever seen. Chinese make-up transforms every face into a devil or wolf, a fierce bird or a giant butterfly with wings of dazzling cloth: purple, silken black, pepper yellow and green. Impossibly long feathers turn people into luna moths. When we stand up and lose ourselves in the crowd and the wind, the press of people and the light make me dizzy: I cannot believe so much happens at once and still enters whole into my brain. Children run among us, shrill with laughter, their fingers in their ears to soften the sound of exploding firecrackers.

The acrobats flip and arch over the stage. Whenever one of them makes a mistake and loses his footing, the crowd claps even harder. Very late at night, the wind howls and blows the costumes into chaos, waving the canopy over us like a red acre of sea. Paw Prasert, Pee-Moi and their brothers and sisters yell for more acrobats. Their faces are so similar I can scarcely tell them apart.

November 16

PAW PRASERT TELLS ME I am going to be in the annual *Roy Gratong* parade. "And you must be very beautiful," he says, "for the water gods." This afternoon, two women come to the house to dress me and paint my face. It takes a mere three hours. When I finally climb up into the fuschia float—it's shaped like a lily—I almost fall backwards because the material I'm wrapped in completely constricts my leg movements. Calf-roped in Thai finery. I am also wearing high heels, mandatory for the beauty contest.

The experience makes for an uneven blend of fascination and horror. After the parade up Yantrak, the beauty contest, the photographing, the hour I spend sitting with old Thai men telling me they'd love to see me in a

bikini, I am thoroughly sick of smiling and bowing and being
. . . used. Ajahn Champa says the Thais just want to see me,
they are curious, but I get so tired of it. After a while—and
a while is about two minutes—it loses its charm. There are
thousands of people in Denchai for the *Roy Gratong*
celebration—villagers and farmers and peasants, packs of
children and scrounging dogs. I switch everything off but
my smile and concentrate on ignoring the impressive
quantity of insects in my hair and down my front. I'm not
the only one under the neon lights of the lovely *Gratong*:
there is also a swarm of mayflies. All evening, I shiver from
the sensation of bugs crawling over my scalp.

So I've been in a beauty contest and been cheered by
crowds. I hope no one in Canada ever discovers the photos.
The Thais see nothing exploitative about it—every girl
dreams of being in beauty contests—and everyone looks
forward to the prizes, crowds and excitement. The audience
throws roses. But mobs distress me and arranged beauty
bores me. While I sat on a crate rubbing my blistered feet
behind the stage, the girls had their bodies judged, even
their fingernails and feet.

After the beauty contest comes a magic show, then
horrific synthesizer music, then a bizarre performance of
singing and joke-telling by transvestites. Everyone loves this.
Finally, quite exhausted by all the staring and pawing and
shouting, I limp behind Prasert, clutching both flowers and
skirt (which is falling off at this point) to the waiting *sam-lah*.
Cinderella must have felt the same way. I came in a float and
leave in a three-wheeled rickshaw. The old man who pedals
it has chicken legs. We roll away at two in the morning to the
energetic squeak and grind of dry metal.

The moon hangs over Denchai bright as a sunlit mirror;
my eyes are too sore to look at it. When we get home it's
almost two-thirty; Prasert stumbles away to his room. I climb
up the stairs to my own, anxious to clean my face of its paint
and unwrap my sweaty, bug-tracked body. I quickly discover

a basic truth about traditional Thai dress. If it takes you an hour and a half to get hooked, pinned and roped into it with the help of two women, it's going to take you even longer to get out, especially if you're alone.

I writhe my way out, tearing as little fabric as possible, destroying all the carefully hidden safety pins. My whole lower body has turned blue: sweat has soaked up the dye from the costume's material. I smell like a printing press. The worst is yet to come: when I go downstairs to take a cold splash bath, there is no running water and none left in the basin. I can't believe it. I would pay money to wash myself. For mysterious reasons, the water is often cut off in Denchai for hours, occasionally days at a time, but this is absurd. It's *Roy Gratong*, and I've done my bit to honour the spirits of the rivers and lakes. Where is the water?

November 21

IN THAILAND, THE SUN HAS SET: the earth arches into darkness and Canada rises to a cold morning. The sky here is orange and purple, an absent-minded blue. The first stars glow; no, they are so big they must be planets. I write in shadow, high on the terrace of the abandoned school. Thirty feet away a stray cat gnaws a mouse. The first night mist uncurls in the valley. I'm trying not to breathe too loudly. Cat: don't crunch the bones. No one knows where I am and I am, incredibly, alone. A man runs across the field below, thumping the earth like a drummer. Nearby a dog howls and seconds later, as though in response, the train going to Bangkok whistles high and long into the night.

Directly below I hear rustling, a shuffle of feet on gravel and a slap of thongs. The ragged flag in front of the old school slides down its pole. *Slap slap slap.* I hold my breath, but the feet pad up the mossy steps. I see the straw hat first, bobbing above an old man's face. When he realizes I'm sitting here, he gives me a toothless grin. "What are you doing?" he asks. "Writing," I say, "what are you doing?"

"Putting away the flag." He unwraps a big ring from a rag and begins touching the keys that hang from it. Only then do I realize he is blind. His fingers run over the jingling mass of keys too quickly for my eyes to follow. Once the correct one is in his hands, he guides it easily into the rusted lock on the door. The school was burnt out years ago and never repaired. Lin and Deh say phantoms fill the hallways every year on the anniversary of the fire, and before dawn the ghosts of the burned students can be heard singing in the surrounding fields. (Ajahn Champa recently destroyed this wonderful horror story by assuring me that those very ghosts are in their twenties right now—not one student was injured in the fire that destroyed the school.)

It is a lonely quiet place, avoided by children and soccer players. The verandah is a high window to the hills and sunset. The walls are charred black or furred with moss, and smell of cats and wild grass. Along the far stone wall I've found enormous praying mantises, giant snails and a snakeskin as long as my leg. Everything but the flag pole is abandoned and going wild. A true testimony to Thai patriotism, the moth-eaten flag remains. The old man shakes the flag, then daintily folds it up and places it in a cupboard.

I get up to leave after saying goodbye to the old man. When I'm half-way across the field, his slapping feet become still. He listens as I walk away. I wander alone on the town's edges, stealing time, drinking silence and the scent of dust.

I've been here for three months: what have I learned? I don't know enough, cannot. I must attempt the impossible: respect everything, judge nothing, keep my self-righteousness to myself. I will never own any of this country, but it already owns part of me. Life is clearer here. Even the language is more direct. I often dream in Thai now. I've finally arrived.

I can't think of my life without these people: Ajahn Champa, Peroontip, Sangkaya, Galianee, Yupa, the children from Nareerat, the girls in my dance class. They fill my days, become part of my own landscape, my thoughts. When I lived in Canada, I was simply waiting to meet them. There is a place on the road where the sun slants emerald through the leaves. At the right time, I often walk there to see those particular teak leaves glow like stained glass. I cannot imagine being without the memory of them.

My feet grow roots when I stand in the market for too long. I think, panicking: I'll never be able to leave, I can't. I forget the rest of the world as I never could in Canada. When I try to learn "war" and "politics" in Thai, Ajahn Peroontip asks me, "Why do you need those words here?" And she teaches me the sugary lyrics of an old love song instead.

For a while, then, I can be forgetful. Thailand forces it on you: happiness, badminton games, roasted bananas. But I don't know how I will mesh everything together when I go back to Canada. (Only by great force of will do I keep myself from writing "if." If I go back.)

November 26

STATIONED ON THE HIGH BALCONY where we hang clothes to dry, Paw Prasert is shooting pigeons. I hear the peculiar sound of his cooing, wooing the birds down off the roof, followed by a blast which repeatedly makes me leap off my chair. Eventually I go out and ask why he's murdering innocents.

"For supper," he says. I assume he's kidding.

When Jaree comes up the stairs, grinning widely as usual, I help him collect limp pigeon corpses. We carry them down into the old kitchen where the dog is tied up; as soon as she catches the blood scent, she begins to howl and jump straight up in the air. Jaree has worked as a servant for Prasert since he was thirteen. He is twenty now, and knows all there is to know about loading crates of Sang Som whisky and plucking pigeons. Once I lent him my camera when he went

55

home to his village for the weekend, and he bowed such a deep thank you I thought his head would touch his knees. He is grateful for everything. If I smile slightly, he'll sometimes begin to laugh and *wai* me for no apparent reason. No matter what I'm doing—coming out of the *hongnam* or washing clothes, up to my armpits in sudsy water—he asks, "Sunook, mai?" Are you having fun?

"Sunook, mai?" he asks now. I'm watching him rip handful after handful of grey down from the pigeons' chests. The dog continues to strain against her chain. I think the pigeons are for her. Naked bodies pile up on the wooden table. Blood drips through the planks. Red streams sliver out across the floor and dam at Jaree's left shoe, which shifts now and then, smudging the blood. The dog howls. Jaree hums, smiling. I go out to the front of the liquor store and look down at the rose garden, hoping to see the fat striped lizard, hoping to see a giant yellow butterfly, any living creature to take my mind off the carnage on the kitchen table.

ROAST PIGEON IS TOUGH, dark brown and sinewy. Or maybe the bird I ate was extremely old. Gritty, too, as though it had consumed a great deal of sand during its lifetime.

Paw Prasert didn't give the dog anything but a few bones. Really I should be grateful. Pigeon is preferable to the latest delicacies I've seen in the market: living bee pupae in the honeycomb, delicious when fried with plenty of garlic, and large beetles with their legs tied together, still twitching. (Imagine it: a beetle whose legs are big enough to be tied together.)

Last week, they encouraged me to eat raw chicken feet marinated in onions and vinegar, but I gracefully declined and fled. Chicken feet! Could they ever replace hamburgers? People here rightly despise *falang* fast-food chains in Bangkok, but is bee pupae really that palatable? Ajahn Champa sniffs when I mention McDonald's and says that their food "tastes of plastic and wet napkins." At least chicken feet really taste like chicken feet.

November 30

A LIGHT WIND DRAWS the veil of fog from the fields. In the distance, crops hang suspended between mist and mountains; the rice stalks are red now, ripe with gold heads. Water buffalo drowse in the ditches under their herdsman, who sits in a tree laced with spiderwebs. We are speeding into Prae, the lot of us, all girls in uniforms except a market woman hunched up in the corner with a basket of red-feathered chickens. Through the mist we see the black silhouettes of burnt trees.

Just before we enter the town, the sun burns away the pale skin of morning and hurls light everywhere. Suddenly, the fields are shrill with green. Colour is music now: a field can be heard. Wind catches in the *songtow* and sends chills over our shoulders. In the truck ahead of us, twenty men holding hoes and scythes stand high up on rice sacks. Their faces and heads are hidden in scarves; their eyes shine between folds of blue, red, yellow cloth. We know they are smiling. When we turn off at Prae, they wave goodbye.

At school, the mad rush for the assembly fields begins. The music has already started, but instead of going to my class row with Lin, I sneak up to the English room. As the buildings empty, I watch the blue-white flash of uniforms, the scissoring of boys' brown shorts. Everyone is standing in the field now and beginning the prayers. When the chant of prayers is finished, the children begin to sing.

I've sung with them so many times now, knowing only half the words, that hearing them alone is like hearing the pulse of someone else's heart. I know I am close, but the beat is still deeply buried. I feel their history, feel the scale of their lives play over my own skin. They sing and sing, and I listen quiet and still at the window. There are so many words I don't know yet. The gift of this place dances around me each day, and I must learn how to deserve it. Sometimes I feel as though my life is an instrument not fine enough for such music.

57

December 4, 1986

IT'S THE BEST TIME NOW, the hour when the light is just paler than warmed honey; if I put out my hand, it would fill up with this sweet colour. I sit on the loading platform at the station, the last train still whistling in my head. It's on its way to Bangkok now, weighted down with enough rice to feed ten armies. The loaders hooked and heaved sack by burlap sack into the train. Almost every man's back was a muscled gleam of tatoos. Sometimes I think the men are wearing shirts until I get close and realize their entire torsos are engraved spirals of ink.

Across the field of weeds and wagon ruts, a raggedy man curses at the teak trees. He is Denchai's most famous, most violent beggar. I am trying to memorize his face, his hair, the muscles wrapped so tightly around his skeleton. If he had white skin, you might be able to make out the exact network of veins beneath it.

I'm not a beggar. This surprises no one but myself. The Thais believe the misfortune you meet in this life results from the sinful acts you committed in past lives, but every new existence can bring you closer to perfection. I gnaw my pencil about the mystery of Buddhism, but it's tiring: one life is more than enough. Though it appeals to me in many ways, I don't want another religion. I am still extricating my limbs from the wheel of Christianity.

I remember some of the distressing stories of the Bible by heart. The most stunning nightmares of my life came when Jezebel was pushed out the window and torn fleshless by the dogs below. I learned why God has to live in heaven. If he lived among humans, he would kill us all within a week. When I read about the great flood, I imagined the ark from the outside, never from the safe interior; they were *drowning*, all those kids and kittens and monkeys. Samson's blind power killed *dancing girls;* I didn't care if they were pagans. And what about the Pharoah's soldiers and horses swallowed up by the Red Sea? Every book in the Bible had so many *victims,* it seemed to me. Even at eleven, I suspected that God was a brute. Falling rock signs in the mountains frightened me; in the winter I felt vulnerable because of avalanches. I knew perfectly well as a child that God could kill me at any moment.

Thailand does not possess a single snowy height to fear. It has floods and mudslides and malaria and snakes, but no avalanches. I didn't bring a Bible. Holy justice is so far beyond me that I don't even try to catch up with it anymore, but seeing the beggars makes me want explanations. If a deranged old god with a white beard existed for me, at least I'd have someone to thank for my good fortune. I can understand needing serious ceremony and secret incantations to communicate with a lunatic.

Instead of praying, I take walks, carrying my notebook and a leaky Thai pen. The people in Denchai are amused to no end. Every time my young friends see me, they look down at my book and giggle. "Will you forget everything if you don't write it down?" I envy the Thais their Buddhism more than I envy any Christian. Buddhists have reasons to be gentle with each other and with mosquitoes; their goodness is merit for the next life. They do not trap themselves in complicated interpretations of The Word, in little nets of paper and ink. Westerners call this simplicity, but really it is wisdom, the same kind of clarity all of us know briefly as children. The Thais do not worship a god; they honour an Indian prince, Sidhatta Gotama, the Buddha, who took off his robes and feathers, scraped away his scales. He became enlightened, lightened, and the Thais bow to this accomplishment in reverence.

But I am left always with one question: why are the beggars what they are? If they were born into poverty for past deeds in forgotten lives, what exactly did they do? In Prae, there are only a few beggars, but Thailand owns an army without limbs, an army of stumbling, flippered bodies. I try imagining what it would be like to live without arms, without legs, but I fail. The undeformed are not so creative: when I am hungry, I eat with my hands. In New Delhi, fathers break their children's legs to make them better beggars. In Bangkok, the masters of beggar-rings abandon the limbless on the streets until nightfall, then collect them like so many weighted sacks of coins.

The beggars in Denchai are not slaves to any Dickensian master. They beg alone, travelling around to the villages in the province, appearing and disappearing according to their own indecipherable schedules. Their ankles are like blades of red stone. Some of them are toeless, fingerless, fish-nibbled by death. I look away and see Lin's smooth face, Joum's violet-edged mouth; I watch the river glossed with sunlight, spilling the voices of women washing clothes. I remember the living threads I have held here: the face of the praying mantis, the eyes of the lizard who lived in my palm, the small Thai girls dancing around me. It *is* a miracle, then, that I walk upright, that at night I slide down to the river banks without being devoured by ghosts.

What is a miracle without a god? Mere chance?

This is what the beggars do. Like warped mirrors, they make me see what I might have been. They show me the reality I slipped out of because I was born by chance in a cold rich country. My skin is pinkish white, uncooked poultry. Beggars are careless with the sun; they are the colour of pure chocolate, much darker than other Thais. Their hair is like oiled wire; a fearful electricity snaps under their skin, scattering the merchants and market women and children away in wide circles. The beggars plunge their arms into the garbage bins, sink their shoulders into the reek of rubbish without blinking an eye. They squat down, grinning in ecstasy on the sidewalks, eating the rinds and cores of cast-offs, getting the seeds stuck on their chins; they gnaw bones which already have been picked clean, they lick out the insides of discarded candy bags. This takes place in front of the marble steps of the bank, where the bin is, and in front of Meh Dang's shop, where there is always a basket of rotting fruit. There are no hidden alleys in Denchai. A beggar's feast is a public spectacle, like the copulation of mangy dogs.

I know the regular beggars by sight. Paw Prasert once told me a story about the vicious one who's there in the field right now. One morning Meh found him sleeping on the stone bench in front of the house. She yelled at him to leave, but he didn't move. Determined, she came back with a broom and beat it on the ground, trying to wake him. He remained completely still. Meh put the broom down and spoke again to him in a normal voice. She slowly came to the horrible conclusion that he was dead. She leaned toward his body, not too close, but close enough to get a better look. Without warning, the beggar roared to life, leapt off the bench in a single spring and jumped down the steps, howling at the top of his lungs, spraying spit and mucus. Meh screamed and cried, and went that very day to the temple to dispel any evil spirits which might have been breathed into her by the beggar's roar. She did special devotions for a month.

When I go out walking, I often see this man. Some beggars have a gentleness of supplication about them, but this one does not inspire pity. He is more a scavenger above the level of dogs and cats. He eats garbage from the elephants' pile in the market-place at night. They say he fought in Laos, and is mad. They say he is a refugee from Kampuchea, and is mad. They say he is from the slums of Bangkok, and is mad. Paw Prasert believes his body is crawling with bad spirits. If you could see them, they'd be coiled and looped around his limbs.

I sit here and watch him, hoping to see any spirit at all, good or evil. He is under the teak trees, fighting alone, jabbing viciously at the air. Nothing is in his hands but I imagine knives. Dust billows from under his bare feet. Every once in a while, he lets out a weird half-choked scream. Now he sits on the ground to rest and cough; the dust spreads and settles like a red foxtail over his legs and shoulders. He spits at the demons crouched so close to him. I wish I knew exactly what they looked like, those creatures he's fighting with, but the shadows under the teak trees are deep in this amber light and I can't see their faces.

December 6

EVERY WEEKEND Deh or Lin or Boh appears at the liquor store and demands my company on the latest adventure. I almost always accept their offers, because they're insulted if I don't. Thais live communally; they often misunderstand the desire for solitude. It does not mean I'm sick or depressed: usually I'm just writing or reading when I want to be alone. But Lin and Deh find it disconcerting to be alone themselves and cannot imagine anyone actually *wanting* to be. After the long days at school, answering the same questions a thousand times, always smiling, obliging, I have to breathe by myself for a while or I end up feeling completely drained.

The Thais don't even like to sleep alone in their bedrooms. Pee-Moi sleeps with the servant girl because she is afraid of vampires. Sometimes I hear them whispering in the dark; I'm curious to know what they talk about so late at night when the rest of the town is asleep. I imagine the quiet servant girl telling Pee-Moi what she can't tell me. Perhaps Prasert has told her not to speak to me. What village she comes from, how old she is, what illness she is afflicted with: these remain secrets. She spits blood. When I rise every morning at six, I find her tissues soaked with blotched designs, red snowflakes and roses already half devoured by ants. She's up at five, packing rice in small bags or sweeping the shop with two small brooms, gliding about with both of them fluttering like moth wings. Gently, gently, she sweeps; the sound of the brooms is a weak panting on the floor. Her long hair is tied back but a bit of it always hangs down around her face. I've lived here for four months and we've never exchanged more than a few syllables. There's nothing unusually striking about her except her eyes. I've never seen such eyes. They're not the black-brown of most Thai irises, but pale tortoiseshell, dappled, almost gold. Pee-Moi says she can't read; she knows no one in Denchai. I wish my Thai friends would take her away on their jaunts into the fields, but that would be unacceptable. She is a servant, about sixteen years old, from another village, presumably a poorer place.

I am often aware, as I was in Canada, that there is another life beyond the one I live now, another level of existence, and other ones beyond that. There is an endless variety of lives from which I'm cut off by the one I lead myself. I want to know those depths and swim out of the tunnel of my own days. At times I distrust my own vision: am I seeing through the layers, do I have a wide scope of things, do I know what illusions the mist and mountains contrive?

Boh comes today and we rush through the eastern fields to the edge of the hills. His grandfather lives here in a small farming community. Boh's mother is a pretty woman who saw beyond her own mother's life. She didn't want to live by planting and harvesting tobacco and rice. Somehow—she refuses to explain how—she made the son of a Chinese merchant fall in love with her, a mere peasant's daughter.

They married without the approval of his parents, causing a great scandal at the time. Now a plump merchant's wife, Boh's mother still laughs at her good luck. "Look at my hands," she says sometimes, holding them up to the light so the gold rings and burgundy nails glitter. "My mother's hands were not like this." Boh's grandmother died before he was born, but his grandfather still lives in the old wooden house set high up on beams. Boh tells me he is the wisest, oldest man in the village now, and I must *wai* very deeply and not let the height of my head rise above his.

When we arrive, he's sitting cross-legged below the house, making chopsticks out of bamboo. Long shavings of wood are scattered over the ground around him. Boh and I greet him, bow and sit down. He is the wisest man in the village because he has the best ears, he says. Everyone tells him everything and he always hears, always remembers. He knows the earth here, the fields, who is growing what, where and how. He knows when the crops will grow best and when to leave a field lie fallow. Around the village are fields of soybean, rice, peanuts, tobacco, corn, turnips.

He sits here under the house during the day, carving hundreds of chopsticks that will be sent to Japan. He is too old to farm, but he feels he must work. One of his other daughters and her husband live with him; he looks after their small son while they're in the fields during the day. The child is perhaps three years old, and sits on a wide straw mat and stares at us intently. After a while, he yawns, rubs his eyes and curls to sleep.

Silk farming is a new idea in this area and the first time some farmers tried it, they didn't consult Boh's grandfather; their efforts ended in disaster. To grow silk worms, you need mulberry trees. The farmers planted three hundred mulberry tree stalks and didn't understand why they wouldn't grow. The stalks were dried up and dead by the time the farmers discovered they had planted them upside down. This time, after long discussions with Boh's grandfather, who once managed a silk farm farther north, another group is trying again.

When Boh suggests we ride out to the field where the mulberry trees grow, I welcome the idea with enthusiasm. I envision foliage which will somehow be related to the luxurious *pah-mai thai*—Thai silk. We politely finish our cold tea, bow to Boh's grandfather and drive back through the quiet village roads, upsetting chickens and a few stray goats. When we arrive at the field, I wonder if Boh has taken a wrong turn somewhere, or if the old man has finally made a monumental error. It seems these mulberry trees too have been planted upside down. They're simply dry leafless sticks rising straight up out of the ground.

In comparison with the lush rice paddies farther down the valley, this expanse of weed and naked stalk is desolate. Beyond the road fifty women hack away at the voracious growth of weeds. It's over twenty-five degrees outside but all of them wear two layers of long-sleeved clothes, big straw hats, scarves and gloves to protect their skin from the sun. The only uncovered parts are a portion of their faces and their feet: as I do, they wear rubber thongs.

Once I am off the motorcycle, the first thing I do is stand on an ants' nest. Before I realize what I've done, slivers of poison slide into my feet. When I look down, my toes are covered with a scurrying red design; I begin to hop and squawk. The women think I'm dancing. At first they laugh but then one comes over, realizes what's happened and douses my toes with her water canteen. A few ants cling to my ankles and must be picked off. I look down at the field woman's own feet. How they work all day without proper shoes is a secret to me. I would step on ant nests every five minutes. My feet actually ache as if they've been burned. Boh laughs hard enough to make tears come to his eyes. When I turn to him seriously and ask, "What is the name of those insects?" he clutches his stomach and laughs even harder. The Thai woman answers me, "Mot dang fai." Literally, red ants of fire.

Returning to Denchai through a labyrinth of field roads, I hold my feet out away from the bike, trying to cool them off. Boh laughs and picks up speed; I grab his waist. "Stop that," he screams, "it tickles!" He drives too fast, swerving between puddles and wagon ruts. I'm afraid we'll skid out and fly into a muddy ditch. I close my eyes and put my forehead against his back. Like many Thais, he smells of freshly washed cotton and Prickly Heat Powder. I'm sure I never smell so clean. When we approach Denchai, I lift my head from its resting place between his shoulder-blades. He would be embarrassed if anyone saw the *falang* girl—any girl—touching him.

December 9

MOST OF MY FRIENDS at the badminton court believe Sak will triumph in next month's tournament in Lampang. Sak is sharp and dark as a whip, almost as thin, all muscle and glisten. I think he would sweat into sheer skeleton if Meh Dang weren't always hurling food at him. "Here," she yells as he's running out the door, racquet in hand, "take this!" and a bag of candy or two Mandarin oranges fly across the shop. Sak is so coordinated that he once caught three oranges simultaneously and asked for another.

Meh Dang is Sak's mother. I met her when I first came here: I knocked a bowl off one of the tables in their little restaurant. She said, "Falangs are elephants!" Then she gave me another bowl of ice-cream. Meh Dang herself was a classical dancer; she does not have a clumsy bone in her body. She can still arch her fingers back towards her wrists and she remembers dozens of old Thai dancing songs.

I don't know how this is possible, but Meh Dang reminds me of my mother, even physically. It may be because her normal speaking voice is louder than anyone else's, and when she talks she cannot remain still. Her fingers and face come alive. Every few sentences are splashed with laughter or "Oh My Buddha!" said in English for my benefit. Sometimes she says, "Oh My God!" or "Oh My Dog!" when she sees me. "It's Kalen Canary!" She has a strange sense of humour, an appreciation for and understanding of the out-of-place, which must be why she's taken to me. "You are very big," she says, "but you have a nice face. We trade. I want your face, your chest, but not the rest of your body." Meh Dang kneads my arm. "But at least you are strong," she says. "Do you want to learn Thai massage?"

Besides running the little restaurant, Meh Dang also works as a nurse in the Prae Clinic, and knows the secrets of *nuat thai*. Every time I appear at the shop, she sits down and orders me to her back. "Begin," she commands, and for the next half hour I receive instruction in the mysterious art of Oriental massage. My own hands and arms ache by the end of the classes. I suspect she just wants to get her neck rubbed and her back softened up, but she insists this is one of the most interesting skills I will learn in Asia. Mostly the "mysterious art" is fashioned of shouts: "There—nono—there! Up a little, to the right. No, to the right, I said! A little to the left. Ahh, perfect. Oh My Buddha, I am so tired." She says that now that I know how to give a good massage, I owe her one every time I go to her shop. Invitations for supper begin coming to me via Sak about twice a week.

Meh Dang's place is always busy. Because she works as a nurse, she knows all the doctors in the small Denchai hospital, and she presides over them like a mother when they come in for supper after their shifts. Meals with the doctors are noisy, elaborate, delicious affairs, with Meh Dang's voice continually shouting orders to Gnop, who works in the kitchen preparing spicy northern food. I sit in on these suppers, desperately trying to follow the conversation, dreading, yet wanting, the moment when someone asks me a question. Then all the attention focusses on me; I feel like a sheet of paper under a magnifying glass. They love to embarrass me and, since living here, I have become quite easy to embarrass. I still can't speak Thai very well and always understand more than I can express, which often leaves me frustrated.

When this happens, Meh Dang says, "Long pleng falang," and I am obliged to sing a song in English. The first time she made me sing was almost as embarrassing as stumbling through my Thai, but now I don't mind it. Thais love English music, the cornier the better, and I've been ordered to memorize a variety of tear-jerkers. Occasionally when I sing in the restaurant, someone walking by outside glances in, stops, turns full-front and stares. A white woman singing "The Way We Were" over a plate of sticky rice and chicken feet (yes, I eat them now) must seem a little odd. Even though I sing out of key and forget half the words, it doesn't matter. They clap anyway and suggest I quit all this anti-social writing business and become a professional singer.

The conversations among the doctors are full of words I don't know, words too long to remember, explanations of medical procedures, descriptions of broken pipes in *hong-nams*, the work of evil or saintly administrators, the drop in malaria cases as the cool season kills mosquitoes. The latest news is the preparation needed for the Prince's visit to Denchai's hospital.

Meh Dang cries, "I do not need the Prince! I need Paw Teerug!" Paw Teerug is her husband. During the week he lives in Bangkok, working for "The Bank." He only comes home on the weekends, sometimes not even then, and Meh Dang suffers his absence. The only time her voice doesn't ring through the shop is when she retreats upstairs to her room to savour her loneliness. I've seen Meh Dang do two things which I've not seen any other Thai woman do. I've seen her cry for her husband and, on greeting him, kiss him in public. Most Thais aren't so immodest—kissing in public!—but Meh Dang scoffs at modesty and says that refraining from touching someone you love is not a show of strength but a demonstration of weakness.

"Thailand is such an old country!" she complains, shaking her head. Once she was offered work as a nurse in the United States, but she would not leave Paw Teerug. When I ask her if she'd like to live in Canada, she laughs, "You are crazy. Your country is made of rocks and snow."

Her laughter stays with me. That's why the shop is always crowded with people, why the doctors come after their long days in the province, why the table is never complete until Meh Dang is with us. She's one of those rare people who wear life draped around her like a blanket. She unfolds it at will and spreads it over all she sees. Even when I can't understand her words, I recognize joy in her face and sometimes an exhausted sadness. Her laughter is a language unto itself and never needs translating. When I hear her I know exactly where I am.

December 16 -
December 31

AT THE INVITATION of the Rotary Club of Phuket, a dozen exchange students from Australia and United States (I was the only Canadian) spent Christmas on the southern island, touring its historic sites, caves, rubber plantations, tin mines, natural areas, etc. Thai hospitality can be exhausting. What I thought would be a vacation became a constant rush crammed in a tour bus full of noisy American teenagers. It had been very difficult for me to persuade my numerous Thai fathers to let me travel alone to Phuket, and once I arrived there, I unexpectedly discovered how much I missed Denchai and my Thai family.

Foreigners anywhere have a tendency to mob together and criticize the people and customs of their adopted country. Some of the people I was obliged to spend two weeks with were over-critical of the Thais and their ways. Their attitudes were incomprehensible to me and I often felt offended on behalf of my hosts. This was the first time since my arrival in Thailand that I had spent any substantial amount of time associating with other *falangs*; it was a prelude to the difficulty I would later have readjusting to life in North America.

But that is not important. What remains in my mind of the southern Thailand I knew so briefly are the good stories of Paiboon Upatising, a Rotary Club member who talked with me for hours about everything from Thai poetry and fortune-telling to mangrove swamps. The following is a collection of undated notes written between tours on buses and in boats, scribbled late at night or early in the morning.

THE LAND AND ITS PEOPLE change as we travel south. The Thais are darker, more Indonesian-looking. The men wash outside in skirt-like wraps of material—what are these called in the south? The houses off the road have thatched roofs, a different construction from northern buildings. Mountains jut out of the ground at right angles and trees grow out of naked rock.

I don't know where we are when the men with machine guns get on the bus, but everyone's eyes widen despite the heat. Suddenly no one is sleeping anymore, but sitting up straight and staring. It becomes very quiet. I don't know who they are, why they have hitched a ride with us. Military men would be wearing their uniforms. Hunters don't hunt with machine guns. I've never seen this kind of weapon before, but a couple of the men stand beside me and I am at eye level with one for half an hour. Formidable hunks of metal.

When one of the six men signals to the driver to stop the bus, the result is communal inhalation of breath. The men jump down before the bus even fully stops. They jog off into the jungle and disappear. We all slouch into calmness again; the bus speeds on.

When we arrive in Phuket, we are met by Paiboon Upatising, a Rotary Club member who has volunteered to entertain us while we are here. The girls stay in an empty house owned by one of the Rotary members; the boys are paired off and sent to stay with different families. We are exhausted on arrival, and spend the first day lounging around. I can't believe the flowers! I thought Denchai was incredible, but here I find the most unbelievable enormous flowers, flowers out of science fiction books.

After the first day, we start touring. In Phangnga Bay, the rocks have gone mad, crashed out of the sea and heaved hundreds of feet in the air, frozen there like hunchbacked giants. Paiboon says they are some of the most ancient limestone formations in Southeast Asia; prehistoric paintings riddle the walls of the caves. Long ago, before the island was famous, a mountain split in two, then fell in on itself. Two long bodies of rock balanced one against the other. An iron plaque is embedded in stone there. Paiboon reads me the poem: "This rock leans like my lover leans against me/as I lean against her/we hold each other up." A jungle begins and ends in the space of minutes because the island is so small. Everywhere light shimmers, light I don't recognize: the sun alive against the sea. I'd forgotten you can look off the glinting edge of the earth and see the horizon curve down.

THE ANDAMAN SEA links up the south, connects the isolated Muslim fishing villages, floods down into the mangrove swamps. The swamps are a labyrinth of roots and mud, laced with intimations of water snakes. From the edge of a shallow boat we see a long-necked bird lift up like a dream, almost too slow to believe. The Thai man who steers the craft through the water is listless, heavy-lidded. I am afraid to close my eyes. The mangroves are cages, row after row of identical tunnels. When I think our guide has fallen asleep and lost us in the maze forever, we glide into the light again, beneath a sky whose colour deserves a better word than blue.

In Phangnga Bay, I swim masked and flippered, holding my breath, praying I will transform suddenly and find gills under my bathing suit. Fish. It's the first time I've ever seen so many dazzling fish, the first time I've ever pushed through a wall of them, felt them part from each other, opening like sequined curtains. I swim in a perfect aquarium. Diving backwards off the edge of fishing boats, staying for hours in the water, never touching earth, I become weightless. Water would make a good country. At night I dream underwater scapes of coral, rock, a rainbow of scales. By day, Paiboon tells me the legends of mermaids.

Later, days later—time blurs here—I wander through the caves, under the great jagged domes, in chambers that flower open inside the mountains. Baboons perch around the entrances or sit out in the trees, watching us with suspicious eyes. They screech like furious innkeepers and their voices rebound off cold stone. The small Buddhist nuns taking up a collection for the monastery tell them to hush. Thai boys lead us by the hand to point out magical stone formations, the shapes of elephants, soldiers, scorpions, naked women. Farther up the paths, I find darkness laid over darkness, black cocoons hung among stalactites. Not until some of them spiral down and fly deeper into the stone mouth do I realize they are bats. Hundreds and hundreds of bats.

At night I go to the breakwater behind the old hotel and sit with my feet hanging over the waves. They beat far down below me, stretching silver over black stones. Every time I hear the pulse of the water, I want to swim or dance.

The sky opens over the sea like an ebony sail embroidered with light. Two shooting stars flare and die out within seconds of each other. Much later, after walking home through garden-perfumed streets, I realize I've forgotten to make my wishes.

January 1, 1987

HAPPY NEW YEAR. I'm on a bus to Surat Thani, dying slowly of heat exhaustion and headache. I went to bed at four in the morning after dancing all night with beautiful Italian tourists at the hotel. I'm sure I'll collapse before reaching Bangkok, where I have to stumble across the city to catch a train back to Denchai. The Thais around me think I have malaria. It *must* feel something like this.

January 3

WHEN I ARRIVE back in Denchai, I discover a decision has been made about me. This happens often. I'm beginning to get used to it, but this one in particular throws me off balance.

They're moving me out of Paw Prasert's house, away from Pee-Moi and the boys and the praying mantis. Just like that, in the space of a day, all evidence of me will be gone from the liquor store. I'm still exhausted from Phuket but Prasit doesn't care: he says all exchange students switch families to experience other ways of living, and my time has come. Still,

I think they could have given me a week's notice. Thais can be maddeningly slow in carrying out plans for themselves but sometimes they think foreigners are rubber bands, capable of shooting through any distance.

I don't want to leave my green-curtained room. It's too tiring, this translation of life. I pack my bags and boxes slowly, reluctantly, already dreading the new house. Suddenly I even miss Canada again. Packing reminds me I'm not a permanent resident. I get the same feeling when I look at the smudged stamps in my passport, the scribbles from the Immigration Department: my life here is not what it seems, not what I'm beginning to think it is, not a Thai life at all. It's governed by dates, the signatures of officials. Moving from the liquor store is a premonition of my return to Canada next summer. I don't want to be reminded. This yank of body and spirit is a small dying.

January 10

I'M NOW LIVING in my new Thai home. Another realization: washing clothes is inescapable if you are a woman in Thailand, and more dangerous than you'd think. You lose so many hours of your life scrubbing cotton against a washboard. It's a necessary custom to wear fresh clothes every day—my friends are disgusted if I wear anything two days in a row—so women must wash daily. Washing by hand is maddening. It's hard on the back and boring, especially the big things like sheets. Buddhism makes it yet more difficult. The head is most holy, the feet most despised. This means that anything worn on the upper body is washed in one specific bucket with a certain brush, and anything worn on the lower body is washed in a different bucket with a different brush. Once you have the bucket and brush thing sorted out, you squat, scrub your clothes to shreds and wring them out in a way that guarantees millions of wrinkles to iron out. Ironing in this heat is comparable to sitting in a sauna.

Even when you hang your clothes to dry, Buddhism is right behind you. Meh looked at me with horror and whispered, "What are you doing?" when she saw me clipping my socks to the rack. "Is that how they do it in Canada?" She clicked her tongue and pecked all my clothes off the wires. She rearranged my despised underwear and socks on the bottom lines, my upper body garments on the top. "The body has different values," she explained. "The rack must be arranged like this. It is our way." I told her Canadians washed clothes by colour in a washing machine; she looked at me sceptically. "If a machine did all of this, it would ruin everything. And what would I do?"

What would she do? She already works all day in the shop, selling fans, televisions, radios, renting out videos. Meh Somjit, I call her, and her three children are my new Thai sisters and brother: Kwan, nine; Boe, the eight-year-old boy; Nong Meh, the four-year-old living doll. Paw Sutape works in the shop by standing around a lot and giving orders to Dow, the pretty young accountant. Pla also lives here; she is Paw Sutape's twenty-year-old cousin from Chiang Rai; she goes to school and helps in the shop. Pla runs through every routine with quiet sadness. She is the first clearly unhappy Thai person I've met.

Paw Sutape goes out to the curb to spit every few minutes. He did that just as I arrived here; it almost seemed a gesture of greeting. He is not a member of the Rotary Club, but the younger brother of the president; he was obliged to take me in because he has a spare room in his house. It's on the top floor, which is a warehouse of boxes. We sat down the day I arrived and he told me, "You will tell me where you're going, why, with whom. You must be home every day before nine o'clock. You must help Meh because we all help Meh. You must wash your own clothes."

And that is what I am doing. I am midway through a sheet; my hands are shrivelled. The true evil in washing clothes is that it's a perpetual task. Thailand is such a dusty, sticky place. After five months, I still don't understand why the Thais always look cleaner than I do. Meh bathes at least twice a day even though it's the cool season and the water at dawn is stone cold. She is out in the back courtyard by five-thirty every morning, washing clothes. I wake to the rhythm of a scrub-brush strumming over cotton.

January 20

WHILE I WAS AT NAREERAT, Meh Somjit changed my room around, moved the bed, the little shelf, and rearranged my small sacred pile of books, clothes and papers. She came up with me to show me what she'd done and to explain the perfect logic in it, the symmetry, the Thai-ness. I saw how everything had been rearranged and just smiled, smiled, said, "Cop koon ka" (thank you). I ushered her out of the room and sat down to cry, not a reaction from sadness but from anger, the next best thing to throwing a tantrum. The same thing happened last night when Paw Sutape wouldn't let me go into Prae with Meh Dang. He said it was too dangerous. I said I made the same trip twice a day in a *songtow.* He said he didn't want to talk about it. He doesn't like Meh Dang. She laughs too much and she is northern Thai. Paw Sutape is one hundred percent Chinese. Though there are millions of perfectly integrated Chinese in Thailand, there are still many differences between the two races. I sometimes think Paw Sutape isn't even Chinese, but a creation from *Star Wars.* Do you remember Jabba the Hut?

I would like permission to move and breathe and speak without having to lower my voice. I'm sick of whispering and smiling and bowing. Sometimes I could almost say I hate Thailand, yet I know that's not true. The strain is in two different directions. If I hate it sometimes, I love it more. The solution is not in being *like* a Thai, but being a Thai completely, which is impossible. I will never wash sheets by hand without gritting my teeth. I will never wear a uniform without secretly laughing at it.

If I could have it, I would take the clear existence. I want to really believe in the ghosts under the bridge; I would love to have the spirit of a mad grandmother following me around, demanding food and devotion. The spirit-houses in front of every dwelling-place, even beggars' shacks, keep the gentle demons outside, away from the people. I would like to place offerings at those miniature temples, even though I see the sparrows and ants eat them every day. But I could only believe so much. I am already myself, used to my own skin. The cultural taboos and catches annoy me. I want to have an easier Thailand, which is absurd, because anything easier would not be worth as much.

January 26

THERE WAS A TIME when I hardly knew Thailand existed, when it was so vague a place I couldn't have sketched it into a map. What, then, has drawn me into the heart of this country? When I go to buy fruit for Meh Somjit, the friendly waking chaos of the market makes me wonder why I wasn't born here. I spend hours watching women grind knives to bone-cutting sharpness; I get lost in the aisles, examining strange varieties of fish paste and fruit and featherless chickens.

The chickens! Their pink leather bodies, heads and feet still attached, rise in such high pyramids that I worry they'll tumble down and bury some unsuspecting child. They resemble those rubber caricatures of chickens found in joke shops. I can't quite believe they're real. I hear cocks crow every morning, dust the English room with a feather duster and then, as often as not, eat spicy fried chicken at night. They're impossible to avoid.

The market pulses, transforming continuously as the seasons change. The sheer profusion of *things*! What do you want? Wild onions, bamboo sprouts, sweet rice wrapped in banana leaves, eels wriggling in plastic bags, huge frogs leaping against their nets, catfish struggling in shallow basins? The other day, the pineapple-seller had a *dug-oo-wat* for sale; he said he would sell it to me at a real bargain price. But what would I do with a grey-green lizard bigger than an iguana? The pineapple-seller said, "You eat it, of course. They are very good roasted." He then explained how to prepare a *dug-oo-wat* over an open fire. Meanwhile, the lizard wriggled below us, tied up tight at the jaws and front and hind legs. Apparently, they can bite a man's finger off.

The market women wear long *pasins*, skirts tie-dyed in spiralling patterns, or jeans and old sweaters. In the cool mornings, some lean only half awake against the stone pillars. Along the beams of the roof, in the corners, the spiderwebs hang in nets thick enough to entangle small birds, who shrill until they struggle free. Some of the women are toothless or gold-smiling grandmothers with flesh like chicken skin. Some are young girls still sullen with sleep; others are already laughing, wide awake, calling my name across piles of green-red ramputan, or gna, the fruit like red and green sea urchins. They ask me when I'm going home, if I'm going, when I will marry my Thai boyfriend. I shout, "What Thai boyfriend? They are all too short and small!" The tomato-seller yells back, "Yes, and men in Canada are too big for us!" She shimmies her shoulders and hips and opens her eyes very wide, making us shriek with laughter.

People come with empty baskets, but leave weighted down by cabbage and grasshoppers and grapes and bolts of the blue cloth used in traditional Thai dress. Women and men and children balance bamboo poles across their shoulders to carry away baskets of *lang-sa* and Mandarin oranges, which they will sell from house to house. Walking with this balance of poles and baskets is an art mastered by children and tiny old women, who bob along under great weight with quick rhythmic steps.

Pink dried squid hang clipped in rows, delicate as dolls' clothes. I find shark, dried or salted, and a hundred kinds of fish flopping in shallow water, silver and red-scaled, or dead in high stacks, presided over by women who brush away flies with fans and loose cloths. The eyes of fried shrimp gaze upwards and the heads of geese hang down. Everywhere Thai voices bargain, murmur, laugh. The market in morning fills me so well that I often go to school without eating breakfast.

January 23

LIN SAYS THIS IS ONE of the things I will be remembered for. I didn't think of it like that at the time.

When I was in my dancing class, Ajahn Champa locked the English room and disappeared into the administration building. After my class, when I wanted to get into the room to get my wallet to buy my lunch, I couldn't find her. I was hungry; I needed my wallet; what did I do?

The logical thing, if you aren't afraid of heights.

I crawled over the balcony and walked along the wide eave to the English room's windows, then hopped in, grabbed my bag and hopped out. The entire procedure took less than five minutes. If it had been dangerous, I wouldn't have done it. If anyone had been watching me, I wouldn't have done it, either—I was in my uniform skirt. But it wasn't dangerous and everyone had gone to the courtyard lunch house. I thought I was safe.

Little did I know I was being observed clandestinely from behind the rose bushes. The janitor—what an innocent title for a spy—watched the whole thing, probably even my underwear, then went straight to the headmistress, who went flapping to Ajahn Champa about the crazy *falang*. Rotten janitor. He probably wasn't really worried about me at all; he just imagined me slipping, disrupting shingles, tearing the drainpipes down, and splattering three floors below on the cobblestone path—a mess he would have to clean up. Now Ajahn Champa is furious with me for "trying to kill myself." She is demonstrating her mountainous disappointment by sighing loudly every five minutes. I have a couple of free classes and am working here with her on some English games and puzzles for the kids, but our hearts aren't in it. She's realized I'm still a savage and I've done nothing to change her mind. I'm not modest or quiet or gentle enough to be a Thai. We are finally beginning to understand this.

Prasert explains over and over: it just isn't proper for women to travel alone or talk too much about certain things. Now that Thai ventures forth, slides miraculously off my own tongue, I do not hesitate to use it, and sometimes I make the mistake of speaking in Thai as I would speak in English. Too much truth is as damaging as outright lies. Sometimes I feel I'm living backwards in Thailand, regressing. What enabled me to come here—a sense of independence and strength—is discouraged in the women of a closely knit traditional society. Fearlessness is not something purposefully bred into Thai girls. Nor is the urge to criticize or argue. Or climb out of windows. If I talk about poverty in the northeast, the exploited thirteen-year-olds in Bangkok, the destruction of rainforests, they listen with amusement and tell me how well I've learned to speak Thai. Only at Meh Dang's, with the doctors and Surapong, the famous lawyer, do I ever speak to listening ears. Even my Thai teachers do not take me seriously. *Mai pen lai* prevails. People drink iced coffee and watch Chinese soap operas. Unlike North Americans, they don't even display a chintzy surface of concern. They are honest about their lack of interest. I suppose they're like most people anywhere, because I'm forgetting Canadians are no different: their own lives are enough for them. Ajahn Peroontip of the long hair, love songs and white lace dresses said to me the other day, "But Kalen, Thailand is so small and far away." And I said, "Far away from what?"

It is a small country only on the map: I learn the world here, learn that countries are constellations, points of light connected by invisible lines, and distance is in the narrowness of the mind. I learn that Thais are conformists, wear uniforms on Friday, have women pattering about with trays of tea, revere customs which I question. I cannot judge that, or want more than there is here. I've read there's even a law in Thailand limiting the amount a person can legally bribe a government official. What greater democracy could one desire? Laws exist for everything, even bribery.

February 6, 1987

THE SCHOOL FIELD IS HALF DUST, half dry grass, still but for two fighting cocks near the centre. Over them, a man sways back and forth; it seems the three of them are dancing. As I get closer, I see the birds are vicious and intent. Their scarlet necks and speckled black shoulder-feathers puff up, their plumed tails whip back and forth. The field is silent but for the sound of claws in dust. The sun is just beginning to throw light over the brick fence at the edge of the schoolyard. I hear the birds growl now, come together furiously to hook each other with their beaks at the shoulders, under the wings, on the red chests. Periodically the man reaches down and unhooks them as one unhooks fishing tackle from the skin. I talk to him for a while about fighting birds. He tells me there is a little pit behind the old schoolhouse and invites me to the next competition.

When I leave him, I walk towards the northwest temple at the edge of the fields. This monastery is large, not like the first monastery in the hills where I met the Australian monk. The maze of paths is walled and shadowed by flame trees and old teaks. I've met a monk here, Ajahn Ramyong, who wants to teach me how to meditate. When I reach the monastery, the Ajahn is eating a breakfast of rice, fruit and fish, so I wander around the temple grounds while he finishes his meal. If the evenings are cool, the children of Denchai come to ride their bicycles here. No one but young novices are here now, sweeping leaves off their porches and hanging up newly washed robes. Thailand will always be the green country to me, but the sister colours come from the saffron cloth and dark copper skin of young Thai monks. Some of them are only eleven and twelve years old, and cannot bear to look at me unless they're in groups and can hide their faces behind each other's shoulders. All around me, silent but for smacking thongs, the young ones of the monastery glide from hut to hut with food tins and bottles of water for their teachers. I often feel invisible when I come here. The quiet activity has nothing to do with me. I am weightless here. The silver morning air deepens this sensation. I almost float up the stairs of the little pagoda where Ajahn Ramyong waits for me.

He is a small man with wire-rim glasses, brilliant black eyes and an almost English wittiness I've never encountered in any other Thai person. He also winks—an un-Thai gesture. He says he learned it from a Sri Lankan monk who studied at Oxford and almost left the monastery for a blonde British philosophy student. But then he came to his senses, mostly because she refused to return to Sri Lanka with him. Later, the Sri Lankan said even a beautiful woman did not make England much better—he is now living full time at a monastery in the jungle. Ajahn Ramyong has been a monk for twelve years, and has travelled many times through Thailand, Sri Lanka and Laos. When I ask him what he used to do before the monastery, he says he has no idea. He can't remember. "It was uninteresting." His mind is a sheath of loose papers, little stories and quotes and bits of Thai poems; I could easily pass the entire day just listening to him, but he insists on meditating. "How will you ever learn to think well if you cannot meditate? It is the first step to developing your brain as a muscle."

I met him two weeks ago here, while I was dropping little stones in the well and listening to them splash down seconds later. He invited me to a glass of water. Once we were walking, he said he didn't want me to throw stones into the well, "or all the novices will be doing it soon and we will start pulling up buckets full of rocks." Then he gave me some water and talked to me about Buddhism, explaining the principles of meditation. I began to learn it in the classical cross-legged position, trying to concentrate on the inward-outward path of my breath for more than two minutes. Impossible. I noticed the buzz and chatter of four or five different types of insects. I felt an urge to scratch my hip, then my foot. Suddenly, I became aware of the ceaseless murmur of birds, distant motorcycles, the slightest breeze touching my skin. Besides all the sensory impressions, I also had to deal with my mind, a flood of thoughts, ideas and past conversations. Before we had even started, I bragged that my powers of concentration were quite good. He laughed when I stopped after five minutes to say I had to go to the bathroom.

Today I learn about meditating while walking, concentrating on feeling only the ground against my bare feet, but it's not much easier. We pace down the paths for a few minutes, then sit to talk again. I take notes in a little white pad, writing long theoretical terms in Thai that I will forget within two hours. Ajahn Ramyong talks about Buddhism and corrects my Thai writing. One of the best things he says is that Buddhism is not the mystical religion it's made out to be in books written by Western scholars. "It is a way of life based on common sense, fine reasoning and the conviction that all life is sacred." The purpose of meditation, an intrinsic part of Buddhism, is to calm one's mind. "Only a peaceful mind can attain wisdom. Once your mind is free, clear, it will be bright. You will reach samadhi, a peaceful awareness."

"Happiness."

"No, no, not happiness. Happiness is not peaceful. In happiness, the mind is moving constantly, and fears losing its present state. Happiness is a refined form of suffering. Happiness is the tail end of the mad dog. The head is the suffering end; if you touch it, you will be bitten immediately. But even if you grab the tail, you will be bitten eventually. You see? Happiness is not the goal. The goal is beyond those happy and sad states, beyond good and bad. The mind can reach above those things.

"It is very difficult for you because you are a beginner. And you are not Thai. You have a Western mind. That is not so important except it means you want answers. You need to write everything down. This is difficult because you won't get any truth out of what I say. The truth is not in the words. You have to go in alone behind the words. You see?" He stares at me for a moment, blinks excitedly and takes a quick sip of water. "Now, pace some more, thinking of the path of your breath, not moving at all through your mind, not watching the insects on the ground. You must try to be mindful, not agitated. Concentrate."

I get up and begin pacing again. My mind is like a closet that has not been cleaned out for years. I can remember pictures I drew when I was eight years old before I can follow the path of my breath for more than three minutes. Everything in there is so cluttered! When I stop to tell the Ajahn this, he says, "Patience, patience. It is not easy. You must let it come slowly. Two days is just the very beginning. You must practise alone, too." Later, after another glass of water and a brief discussion about fortune-telling—he doesn't believe in it—I leave him with three bows and walk back through Denchai while the morning is still cool. I try to concentrate on my feet, on the path of my breath, but the town is awake and pulsing already, and my mind swings open to welcome the clamour.

AJAHN CHAMPA was not pleased—she said it was too danger-ous—but here I am, one hundred miles out of Prae on a forestry reserve with whole troops of Thai girls who are working their way, sweating, towards evening. They drag bamboo poles, Promethean coils of rope and huge canvas tarps across the dusty clearing. They resemble a swarm of ants moving an entire jungle twig by twig, leaf by leaf. The tents smell of dried fruit and ash. There are no groundsheets and each girl has one woollen blanket. The music will play all night and the spotlight will not be turned off until dawn. Ajahn Peroontip is wearing the blue cotton and straw hat of a peasant woman, not her usual white lace. She explains it'll be very difficult to sleep because the ground is so hard and the spotlight will shine through my eyelids. "Why do we have to set the light up, then?" I ask. It's the intimidating sort employed by hard-faced guards in watchtowers. Ajahn Peroontip looks at me, puzzled. "We must have a light for the children who are afraid of the dark." I nod. Of course. Camping the Thai way, she tells me, means sleeping little and eating a lot. "You will never again taste such delicious som-tam," she promises me.

After helping to set up camp, teaching three English songs, and demonstrating how to tie slip-knots and play kick-the-can (a game the Thai girls have very little praise for), I ask about the shower facilities and am directed to-wards the river. "But you have to wait your turn," I am told. Bathing is a complicated operation worked in shifts because there are three hundred of us wanting to wash off the same dust and sweat. The Thai girls wear the traditional sarong-like length of cloth for bathing. They lather up through the material itself and rinse off, never actually exposing their skin. With amazing dexterity they drop the wet *pasin* and manage to draw up the fresh one without getting it more than lightly damp. Hundreds of girls change clothes completely without ever being naked. All that is seen are shoulders and shins. The first time I try this is the last, because I almost drop both garments in the mud and end up naked besides, with little girls squealing around me. It is much easier to wear shorts and a T-shirt. When I ask Ajahn Yupa if I can put on my bathing suit and swim farther up the river, she is horrified. "You have no idea what could be in the water! What would Ajahn Champa say if you drowned? Hmm?" She leans over to me and whispers, "Also, there is a logging camp just outside the reserve." By the tone of her voice, she means there are *men* up the river. I think beyond that to the basic irony of having a logging camp beside a forestry reserve. Very Thai.

Without argument, I agree about the terrible danger of swimming, smile and go down to join the other girls on the muddy shore. They are whooping with laughter, heads thrown back. I see white teeth everywhere. The smallest ones slide down the slick brown banks with outstretched arms; they pull their friends down with them when they fall. Chet and Siphon, girls from my class, shriek us all into a mud-fight. I dive repeatedly into the water to escape splashing mud. After swimming twenty feet through a blur, I surface to a brash rainbow: green banks, sun-painted sky, girls swirled in red, green, purple. They hurl mud at each other and giggle until they are too winded to raise their arms. Collapsing breathlessly in the shallows, they lather up their hair and lean back on their elbows to rinse it out. Someone begins to sing, and within minutes, everyone who knows the song is open-mouthed and flushed. Their voices are the same colours as their wraps of wet cotton. The sun is a split fruit gilding the surface of the river. I smell clay and water lilies and soap. The voices press and fold around me, strong as hands, alive.

EVERYONE IS EXHAUSTED after tug-o-war and soccer. They
sprawl in the canvas shade. Someone has even turned off the
blaring music and suggested everyone take a siesta. It's just
past one, glaringly hot, and dozens of Thai girls are slumped
under trees. I can tell they're alive because hands flap up
every once in a while to brush away insects. This is my only
opportunity; I sneak into the forest, find a trail and follow it
a good mile up the river. No one will see me now. Only fat
bees and black hornets drift among the flowered trees.
Searching for a good place to get to the shore, I almost lose
my shoes in the deep mud. The thought of quicksand runs
through my mind, but I let it drain away. Nothing will
happen to me. This is not the Amazon. There are no alligators or piranhas. If Ajahn Champa knew about this, I
would probably be back in Canada within a week, but once
I get down to the water, it's too late to turn back. I clearly
need to go swimming.

I'm in water so deep it's almost cold. I can't touch the
bottom. The coolness is welcome after the day's heat. Within
minutes, my fear of water-snakes disappears. I swim for a long
time, thinking of nothing, propelling upstream, feeling the
weak current pull at my legs. I stop to look back at the
distance I've come. I find the break in the forest which marks
my path. I flip over in the water and wonder again how deep
it is. Suddenly, on the far shore, I see an entire tree sway. A
chain slaps against its trunk. I immediately imagine a man
in a torn shirt who's been watching me the whole time,
waiting. I tread water quietly, only ears and nose above the
murky surface. Little clumps of algae bob past me. Again the
slap of a chain, then a crackle of snapping branches. I wait,
eyes pinned to the green wall.

I am just about to use the current and kick off down-
stream in a great escape from chain-bearing Thai bandits when
an elephant appears on the shore. I cannot understand why

I didn't see him before because he is, after all, an elephant. He lumbers towards me, his chain slapping his leg (not a tree trunk at all). Writing is chalked on his side; he must be a work elephant from the logging camp. I swim to the opposite shore to get a good look at him, hoping he'll raise his trunk and trumpet or even charge into the water. It would make a great story. Of course, he does no such thing. I don't think he's even seen me.

Slowly, unconcernedly crushing small trees, he chain-rattles down to the river. Every few seconds he pauses, rips up a trunkful of grass and curls it into his mouth. He conjures up visions of a monstrous snail: slow, dull, hungry. Soon he is so close I can hear him chewing, and see the thick skin draped over his rump and down his knees. His flopping ears are dappled baby pink. Once he is sunk in mud, he delicately stretches out his trunk a few feet away from me and inhales a bucket of water. Then he holds his trunk over his head, closes his eyes and sprays his back. After noisily hosing himself down several times, he resumes eating.

Mesmerized by his slow bulk and small eyes, I watch him for so long that my fingers shrivel. I shout, "Shoo! Shoo!" wanting for some absurd reason to make him run, but he doesn't even look at me. I've never been so ignored in my life. I shout, "Arriba, go on, run!" He lifts one foot out of the sucking mud and sets it down with a squelch in the same place. I float on my back and kick water. He does not notice. Finally, I flip over into the current underwater, swimming hard. If I don't get back quickly, someone will realize I've disappeared.

February 12

DRIVING HOME from the camp is a dream of a thousand lives. I sit up with the older girls in one of the loaded trucks, perched on a mountain of packs, blankets and rolled canvas. I can see enough of the world to think I'm seeing all of it. I don't want to blink for fear of missing something. The farmers set their fields on fire to clear them, and red sheets of flame blow in the distance, shaking out frantic insects and birds. The polish of sunset drips down the crisp hills, turning water buffalo and their wagons the colour of wet brick. Dogs fight at the edge of the road and children heave a kite to a windless sky. Tired men carry hoes; women in wide straw hats walk home slowly, loosened by the sudden coolness of dusk, puffs of dust caught on their thongs. We fly along the highway through open countryside, swept along the fringe of other lives by a dry wind. The people I've seen will never know I remember them, that I have them grafted to my memory, part of me.

The one fine missionary in Prae is out to reveal God to those Thai people; he really believes they need to be saved. His blue eyes snap when he talks about "the peasants." I didn't know people like him still existed until I came here. I can't imagine what he wants to save "the peasants" from. When I see the people here, the lives played out in the fields and villages, at the edges of ponds, I cannot believe they need God revealed to them. They know him well, live next to him, see him every day. He sleeps out in the rice shoots with his hands under his head, like a man day-dreaming. The gleam of the fields is his silver belly. The mountain range on one side of this valley is his head and his bony elbows; his feet rise up on the other side. The knuckles of his toes are naked rocks. If he is day-dreaming, we are his dreams. There is nothing to be saved from.

I sit up high, watching as the earth rolls away from the sun. The girls ask me, "What are you looking for?" They stare in the same direction. "Spirits!" I shout to them over the wind, hair blowing across my face when I turn my head. They look at each other and roll their eyes, then burst out laughing.

February 16

SURAPONG THE LAWYER has enormous hands and a voice like the deepest part of a lake. Everything about him is oversized. He has to duck to go through some of his clients' doorways and he complains about the smallness of Japanese cars. "Whenever I drive anywhere," he says, "my knees go up my nose." Meh Dang is making a great farewell supper for him because he's leaving Prae to work for the provincial government of Chiang Rai. There are eight of us in the restaurant: Meh Dang (who is rushing in and out, talking, yelling, singing, carrying glasses and plates, clattering in cupboards, forever a human hurricane), the doctors (who are discussing, as far as I can tell, bacteria, a nurse and the same old nasty administrator), the beautiful female interns (who are watching the doctors like little falcons but talking about the weather), Surapong and myself. All but the lawyer are drinking cold Chinese tea. He sips a serious glass of whisky. We are discussing Women, and he is teasing me.

"But this is why I live in Thailand, Kalen. It is too hot, I know, and the government is corrupt, but at least here the men still control the women!" The doctors laugh but Surapong's face barely changes. His eyes remain half closed, not in sleepiness but in cunning. He is great in an argument. "Pood lehn, Kalen, I joke with you. In the constitution of Thailand, men and women are equal."

I snort. "What's written down and what's lived are two different things."

"Yes, that is true." He takes a long pull on his drink and smacks his lips thoughtfully. "There is a good Thai proverb that says man is the front part of the elephant, woman the back part, the part that follows. You see, though, that the animal would not exist at all if one part were missing."

Surapong has perfected the Thai tendency of finding the pleasant and well wrought in any crooked edge. Perhaps his sense of fairness is warped because he is a lawyer. Meh Dang

91

and her servant Gnop set the table noisily while we continue our discussion about women's liberation in Asia. Meh Dang is making more and more of a racket with the cutlery. Every time Surapong comes up with another proverb, Meh Dang almost breaks a plate. When he says, "Mai pen lai, Kalen, Thailand has come a long way. Thai men used to own their wives as soon as the two married. Now everything is different. Thailand is a modern nation," Meh Dang moans and bangs a dish down on the table.

She says, "Yes, very modern. Women pull logs up hills. People cannot read. A great country. No prostitutes."

The last comment is the only surprise. Surapong looks up at her, then down at the dish of food she's put on the table. "Ah! Very good!" he exclaims, "one of my favourites. Can you eat this, Kalen, or is it still too spicy for your foreign tongue?" And the moment is gone before I'm even sure it happened because everyone begins to talk at once in an orchestrated flush. Meh Dang swoops out to get the fried chicken, returns laughing and sits down. We eat supper talking and chewing bones, eating sticky rice with our fingers, burning our lips on hilltribe pastes of chili peppers, devouring bamboo shoots, baby corn, peas, spicy salads, fish and chicken, all of it variously spiced, boiled, fried, steamed. It is a great, long feast; as they empty, plates are piled on the neighbouring tables and crumpled little napkins sprout everywhere. We laugh as we always do, especially at the jokes about Ronald Reagan, but no one mentions anything about women again.

Meh Dang herself has joked about women in Asia, about Thailand's fame for prostitution. The silence comes only when people are serious. That silence bothers me more than anything else. They will joke, but they do not want to argue. The double standards are very frustrating. My guardians forbid me to be alone with Thai men, almost fall over if they see me wearing a pair of walking shorts, yet their houses are adorned with pictures of naked beauty queens and their weekends in Bangkok are full of frolicking in massage parlours. Admittedly, I don't know how *much* they frolic, but I'm guessing it's a fair amount. When Prasert took me to Bangkok last month to get my visa stamped, we went out for dinner to a famous nightclub with a group of his friends. After supper came dessert: a glassed-in room of bored beautiful women with numbers pinned on their long glittering dresses. They wear numbers, Prasert explained, because they don't want patrons to point. When each man had chosen his woman, they came wading through the pitch dark to our table, teetering on their heels, all shining hair and lipstick. I passed the evening with five Thai "dancers."

While we were dancing, one of them told me she would much rather go with women than with men. She kissed my cheek, which made the other girls laugh. She was eighteen and had been "dancing" for three years. When the music was slow and sticky, the men danced with the girls while I sat at the table eating decorative slices of pineapple and water-melon, squinting into the darkness. I was surprised. It seemed so normal, so typical a pastime for Thai businessmen.

I would like to think Surapong is not like this, because he has such a beautiful deep voice and is so intelligent, but Meh Dang tells me he has a favourite girl at the nightclub in Prae. "Why can't women do that?" she asks out loud when we are alone in the kitchen, talking about men. "If a woman takes a man who is not her husband, people spit her name in the street." She shakes her head wearily. For the first time it occurs to me that she may worry about Paw Teerug far away in Bangkok.

If I think about it too much, I get furious and want nothing more than to leave. It's a strange place. The chaste traditions end in red-lit rooms of numbered girls. In the house, Paw Sutape reigns supreme; when he has his tantrums, Meh Somjit cowers swollen-eyed and exhausted the next morning. In Thailand, it's a fact: women are weaker than men. The law may no longer exist, but in many ways, women are still owned here. Ajahn Champa told me about a Thai king of old whose power over his wife was so absolute that no other man could look at her. She went on a journey through the *klongs*, the inner-city waterways of the south, and when she reached her destination, her skiff overturned. The pregnant queen became entangled in water weeds and her own long dress. She drowned, surrounded by guards who could not help her because to look at her meant death. Ajahn Champa sighs about this, sometimes clicks her tongue and says, "Oh, Thailand." She herself could never be the hind part of an elephant. "I never married," she once said, "because my husband was never born."

February 19

WHEN I GO TO VISIT BEED at the service station, Samat tells me she's down at the house. Usually she works with her husband and the little girl, Poun, stays with the grandmother. I walk around the yellow guard dog, who is very pregnant and miserable these days. I'm sure she'd jump up and attack me if her belly were not so heavy. I make my way towards the old house through a maze of trees and bird cages. Beed's father collects birds: snow-winged, sea-green, red-headed rare parrots, macaws, Chinese-speaking mynahs. There is a blue bird with a long tail which makes me think of a giant paint-splattered magpie; there are yellow, orange, even green canaries, and a kaleidoscope of finches that flutter and sing all day. Some of them also sing at night. "My father does not sleep well without the birds," Beed once said.

The garden is hidden behind mossy fences from the clutter of Yantrakitkosol. A rain of sunlight spills into the courtyard and glistens in the clay water basins, where Beed's daughter stands with a cup in her hands, splashing water over her head. Unconscious of my presence, she continues to sing and toss water, hopping out of the way when it spills silver down the air.

I step into the yard and see Beed in the house, though at first I don't recognize her. Her hair is down and the tennis shorts have been replaced by a long wrap-skirt of orange and black paisley. I can't believe this is the same woman who changes oil and pumps gas and wears shorts in complete defiance of modesty. She pours cooking oil into a large wok now, humming to herself. The door is open to the kitchen where sauces and spices are piled on the shelves, filling several shoe boxes and baskets. Pots and pans hang on the walls; drying herbs dangle from the ceiling. Beed is working. The muscles in her forearms ripple steadily as she crushes cloves of garlic. Only when Poun calls her does she look up and see me.

"Ahh! Kalen! How are you? Where have you been? What are you doing with all those dirty feathers?" She comes into the garden with a boiled pig's leg in her arms. We sit down at the stone table and I tell her about my most recent letters from Canada and an argument I had with Ajahn Champa concerning proper behaviour for young foreigners. She tells me about a recent trip to Phitsanulok. Her voice unrolls like suede. She hoists the colossal pig's leg from her lap onto the table, laughs, wrinkles her nose, and begins pulling out wiry pig hairs with a pair of pincers. Poun comes to her with a butterfly caught in a bag. After cleaning the pig's leg, we make sweet Thai coffee and she roasts me some tiny "egg" bananas: they are my favourite Thai snack. Twilight slowly sifts emerald shadows into the garden, but we talk on about simple things, laughing sometimes, watching teak leaves sail down from the tired trees. I completely forget why I really came to see Beed: to rave about the inequality of women in Thailand.

She walks me through the garden when I leave. Poun trots behind us with her bag of butterflies. As I go up the steps, Beed says, "Be good for Ajahn Champa, Kalen. She was my teacher once, too, and she must be very tired by now, after so many students. And you are worse than most." She laughs. At the top of the stairs, we hear a low, sullen growl. "Be careful of that dog." Poun repeats her mother's words and waves her butterflies at me. "Come back next week to see the new birds Grandfather is bringing me from Chiang Mai." When I wave goodbye, the dog barks an ill-mannered farewell; the birds shrill and flutter as I leave.

February 23

THE MOST TROPICAL PLACE in Nareerat's domain is the library, a shadowy labyrinth of books, ferns and flowers. It is built of wood, yet entering it is like being lowered into a cool stone well; one looks around for the water and moss. I come here because people occasionally leave me alone if I hide myself among the bookshelves. I almost never read because there are too many things to browse through: old paintings of Thai kings and generals, teak sculptures of deer and elephants, a dusty collection of gems and tiny Buddhas. Sometimes sparrows come in the windows, shoot over our heads and careen through the doors, more audacious than the students would ever dare to be.

For the most part, the books here are too complicated or too simple, ranging from *The Life of Mozart* in black curls of Thai script to *The Adventures of Huckleberry Finn* in a simplified English version which I've already read twice. My study of the Thai alphabet is still limited to "Koon Suvit goes to the office every day" and "Noodles, fish and rice are delicious." Writing in Thai is like drawing snails and acrobatic sperm cells. All the letters are slips, curls, twists, back-flips. I've started skimming an old series of British encyclopaedias so as not to forget the English language. (When I reread my letters before sending them, I find very strange spelling mistakes and errors of syntax.) In the encylopaedia, I browse through entries about foreign countries, insects and deep space. "The origin of all life is starlight," I read, and am deeply pleased.

I'm writing letters at an old table when I hear the girls. My first mistake is looking up and smiling. They come sliding towards me in stocking feet, each one a black-topped magnet. Gop, whose name means frog ("because I'm always jumping and eating," she explains), asks me why I write so much. "What, exactly, do you say?"

"I explain what it's like to live here."

"What's it like?"

"It's different from in Canada. It's hotter here, it's noisier, there are more people. The people here have cooler hearts, and laugh more easily. And I have to wear a uniform here, and watch out for snakes when I go for walks. No one skies here. Everyone eats lots of rice and som-tam."

"There's no som-tam in Canada?"

"And no durian, no jak fruit, no fresh pineapple sold on the street corner, no rambutan. No fish intestines, either."

They're genuinely dismayed. Poor Canadians! "You eat a lot of bread, don't you? And potatoes," says the chubby face beside Gop's. "And cheese, they eat cheese," someone else says, and the rest of them groan. Thais have a special aversion to foreign food, and the only cheese I've ever seen here has been that processed rubbery stuff which I believe they melt down and use to patch bike tires. Possibly the only thing the Western world has given Thailand in the way of culinary delicacies is chocolate cake. And a lot of Thais don't even like that.

Five or six scarves of black hair hang over my papers. They watch me write as if I'm performing magic. I must look the same when I watch them loop away in Thai. Gop, the group's spokesperson, asks, "But is there really that much here?" The other girls look around, trying to see what's so interesting in this cave of old books. "And who are you writing to?"

"My mother."

"Why?"

"Because if I didn't write to her and tell her everything, she would think I lived in a big jungle with monkeys, birds and wild men." They laugh at this absurdity, confident of their country's refined and gentle culture. Gop gazes at me. For a moment, she squints, not into my eyes, but somewhere below them; the other girls nudge each other in the ribs. There's something coming in all this. Suddenly Gop asks, "Is your nose plastic?" She is serious; the other girls grip the table and lean their chests into their knuckles like perched birds, waiting for my answer. I look at their low-bridged, round noses and touch my own, which is more defined, bigger, sharp. I explain that it is definitely not plastic.

"Then why do falangs have noses like that?"

In a hushed voice, I explain the differences between Thai and *falang* births. With the help of facial expressions and some complicated gestures, I demonstrate that Thais are born "straight," and come out face up, so their noses are squashed down on the way. *Falangs*, of course, suffer just the opposite deformity, and are born sideways, crookedly, so their noses get squeezed into a sharp point and set that way forever in the cold air after birth. The girls, all between the ages of eleven and fourteen, gaze at me with great black eyes, quite simply stunned. Apparently, no one has said anything about this in biology class. Gop whispers, "May I touch your nose?" I nod very solemnly. She bows in respect and apology before touching my face, that ever-so-holy part of the body. Her fingers are so soft I barely feel them. Every girl bows and touches my nose. One whispers, "But it really does feel like plastic!"

I laugh to myself. Gop is shrewd. She raises her eyebrows. "Why do you laugh?" I giggle. "What is so funny?" she asks. I still don't answer. She narrows her eyes. "Is it really true?"

"Is what really true?"

"That Thais and falangs are born differently."

I make a hideous face and say, "This is what all falangs really look like." There is a murmured "No, no." "Yes, it's true," I say. "We only put our faces like this," I return my face to its normal features, "when we come to Thailand." They all shake their heads and refuse to believe such a lie. "And what's more," I continue, "is that not only are we born differently, we are not even born from the same place!" My voice is a little too loud for the library. "Falangs hatch from eggs! That's really why our noses are sharp! Our mothers are birds! This is a beak!" I say, taking hold of my nose. The girls whoop with laughter now because I've started flapping my arms.

"So falangs and Thais aren't born differently," Gop shouts, having figured me out.

"Of course not! We're all born the same way." She pokes me in the ribs and calls me a liar.

There is a sudden hush in which I find my voice caught, loud as a crow in a box. As always, I'm the last one to realize a teacher is on the hunt. I turn around with my mouth still open, spilling words, and see the librarian thumping towards us. She is old, hates noise, doesn't particularly like the children, either, and definitely is immune to foreign charm. Her thick glasses magnify the natural bulge of her eyeballs. She is an amphibious battle-axe, a two-legged toad with a croaky voice that orders us all out-of-the-library-this-minute-or-else-Ajahn-Champa-will-hear-about-this-you're-all-her-students-aren't-you? We skulk to the porch, shoulders shaking with bottled-in laughter. I'm afraid I'll burst open before I can find my shoes. (Shoes are mysterious things. Twice, I've had my shoes taken and been left with a smaller size in their place. I told Ajahn Champa I could avoid this problem by wearing cowboy boots to school, but she didn't think much of the idea.)

February 26

IN HONOUR OF MY NOSE, the children have chosen a new nickname for me: *noke gaew*, the glass bird, a popular purplish-blue variety sold in most pet shops in Prae. Beed's father has one. They tell me this while we eat mangoes and papaya slices dipped in chili-sugar. Inquisitive Gop is with me again, as well as some of my girlfriends from class, and Dewey, one of the few boys in our group. Dewey often says he'll come to Canada and marry me when he grows up. "Just send the plane ticket and I will be there as soon as possible." Siphon is here, fat, jolly, indomitable, who wants to come to Canada to find a husband who is bigger than she is. Tomboyish Chet is off to the left, rattling rulers against the edge of the chair; she plays the drums and sings at every opportunity. May is juggling limes and talking a mile a minute. She's very dark-skinned, has the sharp small features of a fox, and is known for her sense of humour. There are other girls, too, the quiet feminine ones who breathe words instead of speaking them. They are shy seventeen- and eighteen-year-olds, watching events from the edges, smiling delicately. These girls are too young, too innocent to be sexy—the very word is too vulgar for them— but they are living paintings of Oriental beauty and sensuality, even in their blue and white school uniforms. I've never before seen the grace of beauty that does not see itself. Here it is everywhere. It slips sun-alive as water from the shoulders of these girls.

Here we all are, my friends and mango slices, in the open-air meeting hall, watching butterflies and sweaty boys practise kick-boxing. Siphon has some important questions on her mind and is not at all embarrassed to ask them. First of all, "What is the secret of a big bust?" Siphon and every other girl present do not want to get stuck with small breasts. "How did you make yours grow?" We are the same age, she explains; therefore, we should all have the same size.

They are disappointed to learn that neither exercises, nor vitamins, nor *falang* bread make a bust grow bigger. They really think it has something to do with the bread. They're reluctant to believe it's just something you're born with, or without. Siphon is convinced it can be manufactured with pills, some special mineral which *falangs* take from the time they're small. (I don't mention hormones injected into Canadian cattle.) Chet asks me if my skin is so white because I drink milk in Canada. "No," I say. "It's got nothing to do with biology."

This mention of biology roots up laughter, a flush of whispers and giggles and blushes. Siphon leans over her belly and whispers heat and mango-breath into my ear, "Is your hair upstairs and your hair downstairs the same colour?" It takes me a moment to figure this question out, but a very brief moment. My hair upstairs is light brown with streaks of blonde, bleached by the sun. My hair downstairs, I explain, is black. Everyone is terribly disappointed. Dewey says, "It is terrible, everyone has black hair down there!" Siphon roars with indignation about the boredom of Thai hair in general. "Always black, or dark, dark brown. Never blonde, never red, never anything new." When I tell her that normally, in winter, my hair is dark brown, she is even more indignant. "Your hair changes if you are in the sun a lot. Great. We are always in the sun, and it is still black after all these years!"

Dewey says, "Our hair is different because of the food." He is serious and thoughtful, picking his teeth with a wooden papaya skewer. "If you eat white rice all your life, your hair will be black. If you drink a lot of Coca-Cola, your hair will be able to change colour." I commend him for his logic.

Chet lowers her voice again. "But if a falang is really, really blonde, will her hair downstairs be yellow, too, or will it still be black?"

I laugh and lower my own voice dramatically. "If she is really, really blonde, the hair all over her body will be blonde." A victorious murmur runs through the group. Dewey is amazed. May shouts, "I knew it!" Gop has been silent the whole time, drinking in all this new information. Siphon clears her throat. "Have you ever seen that yellow hair?"

"What?"

"You know, have you ever seen it? Are you sure it exists?"

This conversation will never be equalled in Canada. "Yes, I've seen it."

"Aaah!" This is a sigh of revelation and hope. "Could you get us some photos, then? All the Thai magazines have only black-haired girls. We want to see blonde ones."

I wonder what Ajahn Champa would do if I started giving out photos of *Playboy* blondes? How far does the concept of cultural exchange go?

March 1, 1987

IT'S BEEN A DAY OF STRANGE OMENS. Ajahn Champa says believing in omens is in itself strange. She dislikes believing anything that can't be explained logically in at least three languages. It began in the middle of the night with the scratching noise in my trash-pail. I didn't want to get up to investigate the small creature so desperately trying to claw its way out. I told myself I was dreaming. No such luck. I woke in the morning to a large cockroach on my bed, staring me in the face. It was my own fault for having eaten a mango in my room the evening before; I'd left the peel in the pail. A cockroach will cross a desert for a meal. I slapped the one in my room dead with my blue shoe, sending a spray of whitewash roach blood across the floor. All morning long I had goosebumps.

At Nareerat, I found they had pruned back the beautiful tamarind tree. It now stands crippled in an absurd way, all black stumps at odd angles. Everyone coming to school in the morning looked at it with a twisted expression, surprised by its sudden ugliness. Ajahn Champa says things always get strange before the hot season. Soon the school will close for the two hottest months of the year and people will be dizzy with the heat. "You will bathe three, four, five times a day," she says, "and be sweating again before you even dry off."

Now I sit on the balcony, back in Denchai, looking over the town's rusted tin roofs, shanties, wooden houses and shops. Insects with gossamer wings spiral and wheel through the air. For the first time in my life, I see a small bird catch a large insect in mid-flight, its beak a pair of miniature scissors, its body outlined in gold by the sun. A dry hot wind murmurs to the trees. That same wind rubs the hills beyond the town, lighting the dry forests and fields with random fire. A small orange sun seems to rise out of the half-darkness, but actually it's a blaze on the opposite side of the range. Red streams of flame spring into view and pour down the valley. Every night I wonder if Denchai will catch fire in its sleep. Will I wake tomorrow surrounded by the black skeletons of buildings?

Meh sends up the children to try to draw me out of my quiet mood. I've been working on poetry today, which for Meh means I have a headache. Whenever I'm writing, she brings me some aspirins or has my tiny Thai sister tiptoe up the stairs with the tea. Now Lin, Boom, Sak and Deh all thump up to the third floor and wander among the boxes of fans and Japanese television sets, shouting for the pleasure of their own echoes. Lin's never been here before and hardly believes I can stand being so far away (a floor above) from the rest of the family. "Aren't you afraid of the ghosts?" she asks, looking around. It's almost dark now and they should begin appearing soon. Many times she or one of the other children has asked me to describe ghosts in Canada. I think of the snowdrifts at night, wind howling over ice, the very living stillness of pine forests. Thai ghosts are clearer. They have fangs, bloody hands and silver eyes. As well as living under the bridge, they also live in the abandoned houses of dead people, in the corner of the fields where a young boy was stabbed, in the room where a young woman named Suchada hung herself. "Why did she hang herself?" I ask.

Lin shrugs and opens her hands wide, showing she has no answer. "This is what no one knows. She had enough to eat. Her scores in college were not so bad. It is a mystery."

"Maybe she was very sad," I venture.

Lin looks at me condescendingly. "Sad?" She tosses the word by saying it, turns it into a mere scrap, then eyes me with unfeigned disappointment. Sadness is no excuse for death if you've enough to eat and are doing well in school. Is that not simple enough to understand?

March 3

A STORM at 1:30 in the morning. I might be lying on the roof right now, with this light and wind lashing around me. The curtains thrash against the ceiling, rain sweeps through the screens, and the open windows over my bed slam back and forth. I'm afraid they'll shatter over me. The thunder shakes me to the bones. I curl up without thinking, like a salamander flicked by a finger. Meh's voice floats up the stairs and suddenly she appears in my room. Her pale nightgown blows around her. She shouts, "Are you afraid?" I can barely hear her over the storm. I get up and help her close windows. We put buckets under the leaky ceiling. We slip around the rain-slicked floor, hushed like timid children by the bellowing of the sky. She grasps my hand for a moment, then flutters down the stairs to Nong Meh and Kwan. In the courtyard, long whips of rain beat the trees. How can birds live among those branches?

I WAKE to a calm morning, the ground steaming dry, the sky polished. I feel I've wandered through a jungle or witnessed floods. I don't even remember the storm until I see my footprints on the floor, smeared dust-tracks. Then I recall Meh Somjit in her nightgown, and the setting of buckets and the great crashes of lightning. Otherwise, all physical evidence of the rain and its melodramatic effects has disappeared.

Except for the shop two doors down. When I go to catch my *songtow*, I see its roof has been torn off by the wind. At school, Ajahn Champa says, "That will be the last storm you'll see for months. And you weren't even supposed to see it. Why do you think it came at night?"

March 6

NOTHING HERE is without its contradiction. Despite its long and impressive history, Thailand is like an exasperating child who shows one side of his character, then another, in quick succession. The country is evolving, trying to fit into a viciously accelerating world. Ajahn Champa and the other teachers sigh and frown when they hear about the scandalous things going on in Bangkok: kissing in movie theatres, living together, smoking in public.

When I watch the monks walk barefoot through the streets in the dawn, eyes lowered as they collect alms, I am awed by the tenderness of the people. When I stand shaking in morning assembly and listen to a uniformed teacher harangue a uniformed student, I am equally awed by a need for conformity which verges on cruelty. I'm repelled by the endless rules, the division of respect between the old and young. The boy's hair is two centimetres too long, just grown out of a brush-cut, still short enough to be a smooth-furred cap over his head, but the teacher is furious and holds the black hair in a fist tight against the boy's skull. We glance at this scene in the assembly field after prayers and songs. The coolness of morning is already gone. Sweat slides down our backs and a dog pants among the rows of children. The headmistress's voice, blaring from the loudspeakers, takes second place to this drama in the back row. I make circles in the dust with my shoe. Our eyes hover but do not land. The boy is almost crying, the worst thing he can do, being a boy before a man who seems to think he's a warring general. We are all quiet. The tension is tangible enough to prevent us from opening our mouths. We can only move our eyes.

The boy is obviously terrified. The teacher barks, barks, barks over long minutes. We wonder if he'll ever shut up. "How many times must I tell you? How many times? Do you not understand your own language? Are you stupid? Your hair is too long, too long! It is ugly. You are ugly because of this hair." He gives the boy's bristled skull a good yank. "Why do you want to be ugly? I will help you." He flips something out of his back pocket. We don't know what it is until we hear the blade click out. It's bright yellow; all the teachers here have paper-cutters and often use them instead of scissors. "Let's cut your hair." When he draws the thin blade up, however, the boy, acting out of instinct more than disobedience, jerks away his head and stumbles back.

The teacher has the face of a rabid dog. We see his teeth. He orders the student to go to the tree where latecomers are habitually switched with a bamboo stick. The wood sings through the air and strikes five times. This act is performed in front of all of us as part of the punishment. The boy says nothing, knowing the uselessness of words for a fifteen-year-old in training. He needs his monthly military haircut to go with the brown and white uniform.

I've watched the headmistress make an eight-year-old sob for wearing a black sweater instead of a navy blue one. Once you get used to it, you don't even get angry. It's not worth it. Two weeks ago, for the first time in my life, a teacher wanted to switch my backside for coming late to school. He said, "Yes, yes, you too, the beautiful falang, come over here." I laughed and walked away. Even Ajahn Champa agrees. She says it will be difficult in Thailand until adults begin listening to their children as people, not as inferiors. "Respect," she says, "cannot belong exclusively to the old." She speaks quietly about the child labour in Bangkok, Chiang Mai, the other big cities, the fields, "the loss of minds for bowls of noodles."

I go back to Denchai and see the ice boy working in the

cool, dark shop, wet to the thighs from crushing and loading iceblocks. He's a small, jaunty whistler with bone-white teeth. During the morning and in the early evening, he pedals around town with an icebox the size of a small coffin, whistling madly for strength, followed by three or four skeletal dogs. When he's working, the dogs lie outside the shop in pools of ice water, tongues hanging out, eyes long and yellow and half closed. The ice boy is about twelve, maybe thirteen. He is not unique. The town is full of them. They are part of the scenery—I don't even notice them now. Efficient and small, working children blend into the landscape. They clean, cook, fry fish, flit in and out of shops with baskets and bundles, appear and depart on the orders of some invisible boss. Some evenings I see ten-year-old girls with loads of charcoal walking along the train tracks. They're painted to the knee with dust and their bony feet are sculptures in ochre clay.

March 10

I'M READING A BOOK about Buddhism, the holiness of all living things. Even flies are sacred. I've sat whole evenings outside with devout Buddhists, talking, eating, watching them gently brushing mosquito after mosquito away from their bare arms, while I myself smiled, reached under the table and pulverized the ones devouring my ankles. Some Buddhists refuse to harm anything, even scorpions. All devotion is relative, however.

The sound of voices rises up to my windows. I press my forehead against the screen to see what all the excitement is about. A few doors down the street, men and boys are crowded into a shop, blocking its stairs. They cling to poles, lean over rails, crouch with their arms wrapped around their knees. I leave my room, take the stairs two at a time and slip past Paw Sutape's desk. (He is counting money and hardly notices my departure.) After nosing into the gathering crowd, I find nothing but a small television whose glow has hypnotized at least one hundred men; they spill out into the street, disrupting traffic. The drivers pull their cars over, prop up their motorcycles, and join the crowd. After greeting their friends, they settle into wide-eyed silence, brown arms slung loosely around each other's shoulders.

The television shows a Thai man and an Indonesian man boxing. They kick and elbow each other into dazed red pulps, fighting with the concentrated fury of bantam roosters. When the Thai boxer throws a series of particularly stunning blows, the crowd of men lifts up in one smooth movement as if the ground beneath them has risen; they cheer and clench their fists in the air. But the Thai is tiring and the Indonesian is slowly gaining the advantage, moving in with quick hooks and jabs. When the two men claw at each other in a violent tangle, it's always the Thai fighter who falls away first. The tension in the crowd lessens only when a commercial comes on. Then the men turn and stare at me.

"What's she doing here?"

"Maybe she wants to be a Thai boxer."

"Maybe she wants to marry one."

I shake my head in response to these comments. "I'd rather marry the Indonesian. He's winning." They laugh and groan, but turn back to the television as soon as the fight is back. I slip unnoticed out of the crowd. It's nice to know where I rate in Denchai's agenda of entertainment. Above commercials but below the letting of blood.

March 17

AFTER A GREAT DEAL of undignified begging, promise-making and prayer, I find myself alone on an orange bus headed for Chiang Mai. Alone in the sense that I am unchaperoned—the bus itself is piled with people, boxes, portable stereos, suitcases, two small motorcycles and a bed frame. Most of the passengers are soldiers and many of them are standing. Normally, the seats hold two people, but this isn't normal and everyone travels three to one. Early in the three-hour journey, I changed from a seat to a stool in the aisle because a soldier's hand crept like an enormous brown spider onto my thigh. Sitting on the stool is not much of a remedy, because whenever the driver changes lanes, which is as often as possible, I slide off the sweaty plastic into the lap of a different soldier. When I say, "Excuse me, excuse me," he replies, "Mai pen lai, you can sit here if you want," and taps his knee.

We climb up and down the shrivelled mountains at two miles an hour, but careening through the valleys is even worse. The driver is determined to make up for lost time, lurching in and out of traffic, convinced his bus is bigger than oncoming trucks. Pat Cini, the only other white female I know in Thailand, an exchange student from Illinois, calls these buses "Orange Crushes," and says all she asks of God is not to die in one. Bus accidents are notorious in Thailand. Paw Prasit wouldn't have let me take one if there hadn't been a terrible train collision in which dozens of travellers were killed and injured. Before my journey began, he warned me not to take food or drink from anyone, not to talk to strangers, etc. He's worried I'll be drugged and stolen away to work in a white slave-ring somewhere in Asia. How would they explain that to my mother?

At the moment, the least of my worries is being drugged. The only one with foreign substances in his blood is probably the bus driver, who has been driving all night. His eyes are loose in their sockets and his movements—lighting a cigarette, drinking from a water bottle—are squirrel-like, too quick, *too* awake. In letters, friends ask, "Are the roads bad in Thailand?" Goodness, no, the roads are fine, government-financed expanses of asphalt. It's the drivers who terrify me.

I like these trips anyway. I forget between one and the next how horrible they really are, so I'm always able to take them again. The cheap buses and train rides give you living people and stories. A man in this bus travels with his sickly daughter, who is about eight years old. Her hair is pulled from her pale face and tied with a shoelace. Every few minutes she leans over to cough and spit into a plastic bag. Her shoulder-blades scissor up and down beneath a thin blouse. Her father began to sing to her when the bus left Denchai. More than an hour later, he is still singing, slow deep songs like rivers. His voice is part of the journey, slipping over our dozing heads and spilling into the fields.

The rice has been shorn to stubble, transforming the land from a green shrill to a scorched gasp. Colourlessness invades the country, even sucking the sky to paleness. The flats are savannah; perhaps we are in Africa. Zebu cattle stand in the fields, cowbirds hopping from their backs to the shade below their bellies. If anything moves, it moves more slowly than usual, towards shadows or water. I can't understand why we're so close to the sun.

For the mid-journey stop at a roadside cluster of cheap restaurants, we peel ourselves off our seats, unkink our necks and stumble out of the bus. The soldiers offer to buy me noodles (how romantic), but I decline, drink a few glasses of water and make these notes. Flying ants continually flop on this page and smudge the blue ink. There is an insect for every grain of rice here, flies on the soup ladles, grasshoppers in the doorway, cockroaches basking under the communal sink. Cicadas roar outside. I decide to avoid a visit to the bathroom. After half an hour, everyone is fortified for the remainer of the trip and we begin crawling back up into the bus.

Before entering the Orange Crush, I notice a group of soldiers near the restaurant shack. One of them jumps back, kicking up screens of dust, twisting one way, then the other, as if dancing away from his shadow. The other men laugh, clap and completely block my view. I walk over to see what they're doing. The dancing soldier has caught a lizard by the tail. It dangles and snaps like a live wire in the rain, eyes hard yellow, dark spark of tongue flicking and spitting. When it hangs still, upside down, it hisses long breath after breath, gathering strength, then swings upward, skin rolled on the curving side of its ribs, pulled taut on the other side. It tries again and again to bite the soldier's hand, but is defeated by its own body, unable to heave its fleshy bulk high enough. This lizard is bigger than the ones I see in Paw Prasert's rose garden, beige and black-striped like a species of poisonous snake. Whenever it curls past its own tail, the soldier shakes it down again. The sweaty-faced men laugh and call him a coward.

The bus has loaded up now and I keep looking back at it, afraid of being abandoned in a parched parking lot with this lizard. It writhes at the end of its tail, feet clawing air. The men poke it a few times with sticks. They are impressed by its size. The bus driver leans on his horn for a split second, which excites the soldiers. They are like Pavlov's dogs. The horn honks again. The soldier's forearm is trembling now, gleaming; he lowers the lizard's forelegs to the ground, where it scratches madly at the gravel. For a moment, I think the game is over, then I realize the jerk is just switching hands. Again he yanks the hissing reptile into the air. In one quick arch, it finally swings as high as the soldier's hand, only to be flipped over when the man flicks his wrist and lets go of the scaled tail. Propelled by its own strength, the lizard flies through the air and lands with a thud in the gravel. Blood shoots from its head like paint smacked from a brush. It shakes itself and takes three steps before collapsing. The soldiers do not laugh; they seem surprised by this messy landing and glance at each other with sheepish grins. The bus has been braying for five minutes; only now do they seem to care why. Slapping each other's sweat-patched backs, they close into a tight group again, ignoring me and the lizard. They tramp across the lot towards the bus. I toss the lizard into some weeds and wipe its blood off on the dead grass.

Once I am in the bus again, I discover my stool has been taken by a tiny woman chewing on bitter-smelling leaves. She gives me an expansive green grin when I appear. For the rest of the journey I stand, thinking of the lizard and the stupid soldiers who killed it. One of them, grinning, tries to talk to me about what happened, but I say, "Mai tha-lok," not funny, and turn away.

March 21

IN CHIANG MAI, I stay with Mr. and Mrs. Kongprayoon, thanks to Pat Cini, who knows them well. My room has carpets and air-conditioning. There is Swiss chocolate in the fridge. They even have a sofa and an easy chair. I am surprised by all this finery and do not know what to do with my hands while we eat breakfast. In Denchai, I skip breakfast altogether or eat standing, one shoe on, one shoe off, in the middle of doing up my belt, but here we sit down amicably in the morning and discuss the world. There are glasses of orange juice and placemats. My hosts are wonderful, gracious people, but they make me feel as though I've just come from the farm and still have mud on my feet. Mrs. Kongprayoon ("You must call me Meh," she said after we had supper together) is one of the Shinawatra sisters. She runs the silk and cotton store. She is a very stylish woman, and Mr. Kongprayoon looks like a tall, Oriental businessman from London. I think I should buy some new clothes while I'm here. After they leave in the morning, I walk around the house, touching the elaborate frames of paintings, the vases, the leather chairs. My feet are surprised to feel carpets.

Across the road from the silk shop is a luxury hotel with a swimming pool, which is not difficult to sneak into if you wear the right expression on your face. I swim until my skin is hot, even in the cool water. I spend a long time looking at other foreigners, astonished by their blond hair and bikinis.

It's been so long since I've seen white people. They look strangely similar: pale, sharp-faced, large and loud.

Malay children play in the shallow end of the pool. Their mouths bloom white teeth and sunlight trembles around them in gold and turquoise palettes. I blink refracted light off my eyelashes to make sure they're really there. I want to still the giggling boy with water in his mouth, the girl with slick arms stretched skyward, hair a black flood down her back. I want to keep those two exquisite bodies in this city, and have this day's wind to hook me and hold me still. Time slips from my life too quickly now. The Malaysian children shiver and pull themselves from the water. Their slender limbs drip gold. They are sea animals who've grown arms and legs.

I could hold my breath until I collapsed and the days would still end like this, whisked away in the space of a few words. I am lifted into daylight and dropped into night. The city beyond me glitters and sparks. I tread water in the lit blue pool, staring into the white eyes of stars. I want to be like them. I do not want to close my eyes.

March 23

I GET LOST IN THE STREET MARKETS of Chiang Mai, wander dazed through the crowds and lights and noise. Black-toothed and grinning, the hilltribe people come to sell cotton quilts, silver jewellery and pipes. Burmese puppets and paintings of ancient wars are woven in silk, inlaid with sequins and gold thread. History does not drone here. It dazzles the eye with elephant battles, portrayals of kings who saved cities, dancers captured by foreign armies, brave princes who warred against giants. There are leather shadow puppets and lithographs of men half-monkey, birds half-man. Everything was true once, magic was real, the legends were history, not story. In every shop in the bazaar, secrets stacked up on shelves wait to be rescued from silence.

I listen to a man tell his small son that the wooden marionettes come alive at night. The puppets are courtiers and magicians dressed in moth-eaten velvet. They are orange tigers, white horses, grinning grey elephants suspended from the roof, gazing down at the boy. When the shopkeeper unwinds the handles and strings to take down a tiger, the child hides behind his father's legs and whimpers.

Around me rise terraced mountains of clay and bronze, statues of animals, naked women, the Buddha standing, sitting, reclining, smiling, or wearing a sleepy expression of dust. The light fixture hanging from the roof is smeared with dirt and dead flies. A red-grey veneer coats the heads and shoulders of every statue, obliging the shopkeeper to flop around with rags hanging out his pockets. Whenever someone looks genuinely interested in something, he slips over, whips out a rag and polishes the item. In a row of fifteen sooty Buddhas, only one black grin glints out at me.

I buy nothing, need nothing but the images themselves. I go from one shop to another, run up and down the stairs, walk through the tunnels of stalls where sellers eat while standing up, scooping noodles into their mouths with chopsticks and heroic concentration. Luminous rows of silver, gold, burnished bronze, copper bracelets catch my eyes. Jade sprawls in snake-green loops. Ancient coin collections, strange contraptions for smoking opium, monster-face masks made of wood and glass hang on the walls. Ropes of semiprecious stones rattle when the wind sweeps through the stalls: garnet, lapis lazuli, tiger's eye, topaz, jet. Gnome-like men try to sell "genuine Burmese sapphires and diamonds" for ridiculously low prices. The sincerity in their faces is equalled only by the falsity of their gems, which have all the enticing glitter of dimestore rings. I haggle for the sake of haggling, only to walk away when they lower their prices. Their pleading voices are stamped out by the footsteps of the crowd. Voices meet in warm off-beat waves, crashing together, then washing out again.

I see Germans, Americans, Scandinavians. The German women are scandalous in their braless T-shirts and dirty shorts, stalking through the mass, eyes like blue glass above their sunburnt cheekbones. They seem a different species altogether.

I rove around the market, retracing my steps, lost in the surge of new people. Men on the streets make paper snakes slither into life. Street musicians play bamboo flutes and out-of-tune guitars. Suddenly the hot wind leaps up; women yelp and catch their long hair. The hanging silver becomes wind chimes; the suspended puppets wriggle their legs. Everyone moves quickly, lightly, struck by this wind as if by a match. I meet as many eyes as I can and smile.

When I start to walk back to the Shinawatra shop, it's already very late. The streets are strange to me; I walk around in circles many times before finally getting some sense of direction. I pass numerous temples, or the same temple numerous times on different sides, and I am always surprised. In daylight, the fretted glasswork is a brash array of colour, but darkness turns the spectrum into a strange, glittery grey. Suddenly, staring up at one of these ghostly temples, I feel exhausted. I hail a *songtow* to take me back to the silk shop. The driver squints at me. "The shop won't be open now," he says. "It's too late." He thinks I'm a desperate tourist, off to buy silk at one in the morning. "Yes, I know that, but I want to go anyway." I hop in the back. He sits in the driver's seat, not even looking at me through the back window. I bang on the roof. Bang again. He puts the little truck into gear, shaking his head.

We arrive. "Are you sure you don't want to go to the hotel?" he asks. "Yes, positive," I say, paying him the fare. He shoots one look back over his shoulder as he roars away, eyes saying, "Crazy falangs." The house is set back from the shop, nestled in a grove of fruit trees. I walk to the gate, which plainly tells me I've stayed out too long: it's locked. I throw my shoes into the yard, hook myself onto the top rail and struggle up. Once balanced on top, I look around to see if I'm being watched—this skirt was not designed for such acrobatics—then swing my legs around to the other side and drop into the grass without tearing any clothes or ligaments.

I tramp barefoot through the dew, impressed by the ghostly white woman, classical Greek, gazing at me from a pedestal. She is a little out of place in Siam, but not without charm. I think vaguely about the imported chocolate in the fridge. Just when I realize I'm quite hungry, I see the dog coming for me at a steady lope, teeth and chain flickering under the yard light. He doesn't even bark, just barrels across the yard with his teeth bared, feet beating hard on the wet grass. It's almost like something filmed in slow motion, the graceful swell and fall of his shoulder muscles. I look back at the gate, but it's too far. I would never make it over in time.

It's true. Your life does flash before your eyes. Not event by event, of course—that would take too long—but more like a kaleidoscope hurtling through your skull and down your spine. It explodes near your tail-bone and you either move or die.

I scramble at the fence, slipping, knowing the dog is just there behind me, ready to sink his teeth into my calf. I glance open-mouthed over my shoulder and think I'm dreaming. He's stopped in his tracks about two metres away. He is growling, yes, and barking now, half-snorted hackle-raising barks, but he is not chewing off my leg. His black lips wrinkle back over his jaws. My heart thumps in my chest like a jackrabbit.

Then I hear an amiable voice come from the trees. "Sawatdee-crup," says the night watchman, hat in hand. "Good luck I had the whistle," he says with a laugh, dangling a slender shiny tube in the air. He swings it around on the chain a few times and slips it into his pocket. He calls back the dog and scratches it behind the ears for a moment, then grins at me. His teeth are also very white. "You go in to get some sleep now, no?" I nod, smooth out my skirt, pick up my shoes.

I learn later that the dog's name is Dino. From the Flintstones.

March 26

I'VE BEEN INVITED to a Bangkok Rotary Club conference, but I think I'm too hot to leave Chiang Mai. Pat and I go swimming during the day, or read at the American Alumni library, or walk through the markets, mesmerized by merchandise and the blind singing beggars. The beggars wander or stand still in the throng, mouths and puckered eye-sockets gaping, cups held out. Their songs are unintelligible but riveting. The beggars remind me of fanatics speaking in tongues, or of suffering lunatics from mediaeval madhouses. They stand or crouch in the streets and wail like human ravens. I don't know whether to cry with them or put my fingers in my ears and rush away. There are others, too, those with bloody stumps and open sores, those who cannot be acting, legless men who drag themselves towards your feet. Bubbly-skinned women lean on the walls, children sprawling over their tangled legs. Their faces are exquisite studies in misery. A few baht coins will not save anyone, but I don't know what else to do. Pat continually tells me not to give money to the beggars, not to talk about them.

It is above forty degrees these days, even in the shade. I can't live here. My brain is boiling inside my head. I think longingly of snow. I take cold showers and get out of them sweating. This is one reason why I'm not going to Bangkok, even though I have some good friends there, including Suradev, who resembles Buddha's son and has the most beautiful hands. I will not go because I'll have to stay in a cheap hotel with bad air-conditioning and no washing machine. I'll have to wash clothes by hand every day. It will be even hotter there than it is here. The crappy little hotel will have cockroaches and sleazy tourists coming and going constantly with Thai prostitutes. I'll eat nothing but noodles and fruit from the street-vendors. I'm not going.

March 29

I'M ON A THIRD-CLASS TRAIN, Chiang Mai to Bangkok. There
are mostly men and small cockroaches in this coach, and the
tendency in both species is to slide towards *falangs.* One man
lies down on the floor and puts his feet up against the
wall—until he sees me staring at him. He lowers his unholy
feet apologetically and curls up in a sweaty ball. I've given
up sleep. I stare out at the black fields and red-striped hills.
Fires like streams of lava melt down into the valleys. When I
open the window and lean into the hot winds, black shadows
flutter down to my arms. Thinking only of poisonous insects
or blood-sucking bats, I shriek, then realize I've been stung
by live sparks of ash.

Pushing the window up again, I see the perfectly reflected
image of the opposite aisle. I meet the blinkless gaze of six
panthers, Thai men, twelve eyes touching mine in the
window. They grin occasionally, faces shining, cigarettes in
their mouths. Their fingers are the blunt, blackened fingers
of mechanics or metal workers. It's about three in the
morning. One of the few women in the coach sleeps on the
floor ahead of me, one hand thrown up on the bench,
clutching her daughter's ankle. The little girl's knees are
drawn up to her chest and her head rests on a folded bundle
of cardboard. I trade yawns with my reflection in the window,
but sleep is still out of the question. Everything I see becomes
the dreams I'm supposed to be having right now. At each
stop in each dirty train station, I think I hear a woman
singing or a child crying. Beggars and bums with rag-bags
sleep on the station benches. They do not stir as we pass.

At Phitsanulok someone throws a wadded napkin at me
through the window: a name, address, phone number, and
"I lov YU" written in small letters. I laugh. The train boys
come in to sell warm water, stale food, contraband cigarettes
and questionable condoms. I laugh again, especially when I
recognize one of them from Denchai. He is surprised and

happy to see me here; we greet each other warmly and talk about our families before he begins his act. He is as good as a professional mime artist, but better because he is really a tired seventeen-year-old vendor in a dirty uniform. He demonstrates why I should take up smoking, presenting a Joan Crawfordish vamp with sucked-in cheeks and fluttering eyelashes. Then he encourages me to buy some sweet milk to cure my parched throat. He mimics a baby suckling a mother's immense breast, shows me how strong the baby is afterwards. The condoms, he explains with great embarrassment, are really party balloons, nothing more. I buy a bottle of water. He does an absurd little dance when I give him the money, then heads off to the next coach with his partner, a younger fellow who has not stopped yawning and rubbing his eyes since he appeared.

Behind me, two other women in the car are wakening. They are old and heavy ladies, who groan and complain as soon as they open their eyes. They launch into a discussion about old bones and bad backs. This immediately attracts the attention of a few gentlemen who can't sleep, either; they've been discreetly draining a mickey of Mekong whisky instead. In the course of the conversation among this little group, one woman coyly reveals that she is an accomplished masseuse. The other (who chews a wad of betel-nut leaves the size of a ping-pong ball) is a palm-reader. The masseuse starts giving one of the old men an impromptu massage, kneading his upper shoulders and shaking her head gravely. "Kang, kang mot leu-ey!" she groans, indicating the rock-hardness of the man's back. He takes a swig of Mekong with some difficulty. The masseuse pounds away now, and the bottle will not stay still on his lips. On the opposite seat, the betel-nut chewer reads a palm. She squints at the lines of destiny and croaks in a low voice, then leans excitedly towards the wrinkled hand as though she might lick it.

I wonder where Bangkok is. Shouldn't it be here by now? Shouldn't the city lumber out of the rice fields soon?

Bangkok always comes to you slowly, languidly, but its sprawling outskirts gradually transform into a taloned, grinning creature with an appetite for money and human time. I've grown used to the dimensions of Denchai, the familiar streets of Chiang Mai, the cotton clothes and rubber thongs of small towns. The pace of the city always surprises me. Slums trip into office buildings, apologizing with flimsy fences; markets wander into streets, shopping centres into dirty sky. Concrete edges elbow ancient temples, nudge palaces for room to grow, expand, swallow up the old to spit out the new. I dig through my knapsack for what's left of my wristwatch. The crystal is cracked and the second hand doesn't work, but it tells me the time: four-thirty. The city is still two hours away, yawning in the dark.

April 3, 1987

THANKS TO JOHN TYLER and his wife Dede, I've been rescued
from Cockroach Haven and taken to live in luxury after less
than two days of washing clothes in the sink. I met Mr. Tyler
at the Rotary conference and he invited me to stay with him
and his family. Now I am in a high-rise luxury apartment with
my own private bathroom. A swimming pool on the lobby
floor is visible if I lean over the balcony. If we weren't up so
high, I could jump in.

Dede Tyler is a beautiful, white-haired, Italian-American
woman, and John Tyler a fatherly engineer from Texas. Of
course, he is in the oil business; his company has offshore
drilling operations in southern Thailand. Their son Brian
studies at the American school and wants to learn to speak
Spanish. They are passing through, though they've been
here for almost a year and will be here for at least one more.
Bangkok is a kind of Oriental New York to them. I experience the same jarring sensation I felt in Chaing Mai when
I stayed with the Kongprayoon family and their carpets.
Here it's many times worse, this feeling of not belonging.
The crackers and the cupboards full of American cereal

disorient me. It's an American kitchen, not a hardwood cutting table, water basin and leaky hose. In the *falang* refrigerator, which I open too often, there are all kinds of delicacies: cheese, mayonnaise, mustard, sliced ham, a leftover piece of pizza. Pizza. I am whispering "Cornflakes" to myself when Libby comes in. She is the Thai servant. I wonder vaguely where she got the name "Libby." It doesn't sound very Thai to me. She can speak English, but I talk with her in Thai.

"Are you really so surprised to see all these falang foods?"

"I'm just not used to it yet."

"What?"

"The house of falangs."

"But you live with your parents, don't you?"

"Yes, my Thai parents. But my real parents live in Canada. I live in Denchai."

"Denchai?"

"It's in the province of Prae."

"You live in Prae? Prae?" Incredulous, she looks up at me from the chopped carrots. "But there are no falang toilets in Prae!"

"There are a few. Not in my house, though. A falang can live without a falang toilet."

She laughs. "I can't even live without a falang toilet, Miss Kalen."

"No, no, just call me Kalen."

She turns on the cold water. "Why don't you live in Bangkok or Chiang Mai? Why not a city?"

"Because I wanted a small town, not too many people."

She nods slowly, smiles. "Do you eat sticky rice every day?"

"I usually do, yes, when I eat lunch with my friends at school." Sticky rice is typical northern Thai cuisine.

"Aaah! Then you should be very careful or your nose will go flat like the hilltribe people's. You will start wearing bells on your clothes and believing in spirits." She jokes now, as many southern Thais do, about the provincialism of the north. I tell her it's too late, I already do believe in spirits. She laughs.

We spend the rest of the morning in the kitchen, she peeling vegetables and cleaning fish while I sew up my knapsack. The kitchen is the most comfortable place for me. Though the entire apartment is beautiful, finely decorated, touched everywhere with "home" details, I am uncomfortable here.

Later in the day, the Tylers and myself eat dinner at a polished oak mirror, complete with crystal salad bowls, lovely plates and real napkins. No one puts the bones on the table. Libby serves us. We talk of pleasant, interesting things, the American women's club, the university Brian will go to in the States, my "experience" in Denchai. There is confusion about my intentions. "Thai isn't a very practical language, is it?" asks Dede. "Thailand's a bit out of the way, isn't it?" says Mr. Tyler. "That was the idea," I explain. They nod frequently. We are very polite. I am genuinely thankful to these people for their hospitality, their kindness, yet sometimes when I smile I am acutely aware of my teeth and nothing else. Libby pads in and out with the French dressing, the ice water, the wine. (Wine! Culture shock!)

In the evening, we watch videotaped versions of "Sixty Minutes" and "Dallas." For the first time in eight months, I hear the voice of Dan Rather and feel profoundly ill and guilty. I have forgotten the world here. I have forgotten cloth napkins and political slaughters taking place in the Middle East. I have completely forgotten the IRA, the hole in the ozone layer and the contamination of the ocean. I once wrote irate letters about all those topics. That world has faded here. With some difficulty, I get out of the easy chair, excusing myself, grinning my "goodnight" with as much sincerity as I can muster. I don't think my stomach would make it through "Dallas."

What is it? What's wrong with me? Bangkok *is* an Oriental New York, there should be foreigners here, sweeping gracefully past Thailand and its language. It is the order of things, the swimming pool, the potted plants, the chauffeured car, the marble patio all attended and cleaned by Thais who say "mister, madam, miss, sir." The natives patter after the whites, help them, negotiate traffic, shop for them, cook their meals with delicate spices, open and close their fine curtains. I should not care about this. I am a *falang*, too, no matter how doubtful that seems. I am one of them, I think, surprised I'm calling North Americans "them." I sit in the dark and think about it reasonably. I would give up my life to have a Thai's life. Is that reasonable? Certainly. I believe the trade would be worth it. I would stop thinking so much. I would simply live with normal human doses of happiness and sadness, but clearly.

What I am now is an interesting deformity. I am not Asian and never will be. Even if I forget it sometimes, no one else does. I am the wrong colour. But I am not what I was before I came here, either. Something in me has changed, or grown. If a word exists that describes this quality, I don't know it. So many words in Thai contain the word "heart": *sow-jai, mun-jai, ron-jai, dee-jai, jai-kang, jai-dee, cow-jai, toke-jai, jai-eng* . . . sadness, gentleness, anger, happiness, coldness, kindness, understanding, surprise, self are all expressed in terms of the heart. If there were a word to explain what has happened to me here, it would be a "heart" word, and it would be Thai.

I have to concentrate when I speak to the Tylers. I have to stop myself from *wai*-ing and taking off my shoes before I go into the house. I've been with them for three days in their happy Western home and I keep shutting myself in the bathroom to cry. I am in Bangkok and I miss Thailand. I miss the little town in the north that exists only because the railway runs through it. I miss my Thai fathers asking me if I've eaten yet, where I'm going, from whence I've come, whether I can manage a certain spicy dish. I even miss fried fish intestines.

April 6

THE DIRTY STREETS are refuge from the immaculate house. I walk along Sukhumvit at dusk, when the heat simmers down to a calm bubbling. The air is mostly smog but I gulp it anyway and walk too fast, letting my eyes slip into everything. The street is famous for its profusion of fake merchandise, everything from twenty-dollar Rolex watches to three-dollar Lacoste shirts and socks. If it can be paid for, it can be found in Bangkok. The people of the streets are familiar to me. The fruit-sellers are the same women in Denchai, smiling and clapping their hands over jokes, rubbing baby powder on their children's faces, complaining eternally about the heat. The shoemaker works with a lowered head and solemn face, half buried in a mountain of reeking rubber, hardening tar, shoenails, old soles. Children scurry out into the traffic to sell roses and jasmine wreaths, dispensing these fragrant delicacies while their own lungs blacken with car exhaust. Beauty and filth walk side by side, passing each other sometimes but always meeting again.

The shops spill their counterfeit goods into the street. Men and women try to sell me Gucci wallets for a few dollars, all telling me they have a special deal just for me. Music from five different stereos drifts or jerks through the air, disappearing in the roar of traffic horns, hurtling trucks and mad *tuk-tuk* drivers. A wizened man wants to sell me a stuffed cobra and mongoose, "locked in precisely this death-grip when they killed each other." The cobra might be a touched-up garter snake and the mongoose a scruffy weasel, but the old man says, "Nonono, this is Genuine King Cobra." However, if it really doesn't interest me, he also has canes carved of animal bones, monkey skulls, elephant-hide boots. . . .

I walk grinning through this clamour, wondering if it's possible after all. Is there some kind of operation to take the high glass-bird bridge out of my nose? Should I just eat more sticky rice? Is there a pigment to properly darken my skin? I would do it without question, without a moment's hesitation. This is my country, or would have been if I could have chosen. I stride through the tumult of people, each step longer and lighter, the racket of the streets around me. A bird beats its wings in my body, half lifting me off the ground, trying to escape.

April 9

THE FORTUNE-TELLERS on the top of the Muh Boon Klong shopping centre are unscrupulous. They sit at their desks with complex diagrams and charts, whispering all kinds of fantastic tales of disaster and success. They blend sincerity, lies and psychology with such art that one can't help wondering if they might *really* know how to foretell the future. Two girls are beside me now, almost in tears, watching the supple dance of a palm-reader's finger over a pale hand. Though I can't hear what he tells them, they huddle together in an attitude of suffering, following the tragic lines of the one girl's palm.

My fortune-teller is an old man with a three-inch hair curling out of a mole on his chin. Once he has my palm, he won't let me go. How many lines can one palm possibly have? Is he reading the fingerprints, too? He tells me I'll live a long time and will survive a terrible accident when I'm about sixty. I'll marry a rich older foreign man when I'm twenty-two and have three children. I laugh at this. I'm never getting married. He gazes up at me with a yellow eyeball. "Why do you laugh? Do you not believe me?" I assure him I take everything he says seriously. He adjusts his little lamp and gets out a magnifying glass to read the fine print. "Aaah, how sad. You will never have much money. It will always go in and out, ley-aye leu-aye, like a tide." He turns away for a moment to blow his nose, one hand still holding mine, then squints down again at my palm. "You will always be unsettled, doing too much. You don't understand jai yen yen." He looks into my face. "How long will you stay here?" I tell him about five more months. He clicks his teeth. "You should stay longer." He sighs and shakes his head, then focusses on a point on my face, coming so close that I lean back too far and almost fall off my stool. He still hasn't let go of my hand. "That mole there, that little one by your nose." I touch it. "It's got to go," he orders. "It's terrible to have a mole like that. I know a doctor who will remove it very cheaply."

"Why should I remove it?" I touch the little black dot again. The doctor who'd remove it is probably his brother-in-law.

"You must cut it out immediately." There is great urgency in his voice. He tightens his sweaty grip on my hand. "That mole is in the line of tears," he whispers. "It will draw tears out of your right eye continually. You will cry so much just because mole is in such a sad position." I extricate my fingers with the excuse that I have to find my money. He says, "You have very hard hands for a woman." I put his fee down on the desk with a clatter; a few coins roll away. When he jumps up to get them, I stand. "No, no, wait a moment. Don't you want to meet the doctor who will remove that mole for you?" He reaches for my hand again, but I'm already moving into the crowd of people, hurrying, rubbing the feeling of his hand off my palm.

April 9

BANGKOK SINKS EVERY YEAR because of its *klongs*, the living waterways that once flourished in every part of the city. Many of them have been filled in now, replacing the glide of boats with the snort of traffic, but some of them still wind away from the edges of the city. A man with purple tattoos on his shoulders takes me out in his long boat, promising me he knows his way. He says he's lived all his life on the water of this city.

He pushes us away from the dock once I am sitting up in the bow. "Don't fall in," he warns and sways the boat with a laugh. We slip quickly out of sight of Bangkok into the labyrinth of canals. I feel like a lazy explorer, sun hot on my face, hands trailing in the water to make sure it's really there. There is a whole new country on the water, a different kind of life, but I only glimpse it as we glide away. The small motor hums and a light spray hits my arms and neck.

Houses on stilts stand off the banks, linked to each other by rambling bridges and long wooden walkways. The people live on and in the water, bathing, washing clothes, cleaning pots. Skiffs poke narrow noses through water lilies and hyacinth, tapping ribs with each other when their owners stop to chat or sell fruit and vegetables. I see a tiny craft piled high with watermelons. People lean out windows and wave. Shrunken as an old apple, a small woman works her way up the mud steps of the shore, shrivelled feet bare, a cane balancing her ascent. As we go by, she turns and smiles, her mouth full of gold teeth. On the porch above her, two small children and a dog race back and forth in a game of tag.

I lose count of the women I see bathing in hip-deep water, flowered *pasins* and arms gleaming, hair lathered white with shampoo. Children swim around them like dolphins. Half-naked boys fly off the docks and porches, shouting battle cries and smacking in curled-up balls into the water, in competition for the biggest splash. Slick brown, they flip and turn over with the agility of seals, then scramble up the ladders to begin again.

We are in the *klongs* for a long time, possibly two hours, sliding deeper and deeper into the country. I don't know where the city is. I see nothing familiar, nothing but *klong*, wooden houses knee-deep in water, glossy plants on the shores, Thai faces. I'm beginning to suspect that in my tattooed boatman I've finally encountered the evil Thai man Paw Prasit always warns me about, the one who is going to steal me away. I glance back at him. He grins and sucks on his cigarette. "It's almost finished," he says.

"But where's the city?"

"What do you mean, the city? It's right over there." He gestures towards the mouth of another *klong*, the same kind we've been travelling through for two hours. I'm sure the city is in the opposite direction. I begin to worry. I feel dizzy, too, light-headed. We hum around one curve, then another, both so long and gradual I hardly know they're curves. We turn down a different canal and suddenly, when I look across the river, the skyline of Bangkok looms before me. I glance back down the *klong*, baffled by the quick materialization of the city. "I told you I knew where I was going," says the boatman. He manoeuvres us to the opposite shore, passing bigger boats, junks and rafts, waving at people he knows.

"Wait a minute, this isn't the same place. I don't know the way back from here," I protest. "I have no idea where I am."

He gets out onto the dock and offers me his hand with a weary sigh. "All you have to do is go up the stairs, cross the bridge, cross the street, and catch the number twenty-two bus back. Where you going from there?"

"To an apartment on Sukhumvit Road."

"Hmmm. Well, maybe just catch the number seven." He hesitates. "Or the number seventeen? Anyway, just get on a bus and you'll find your way home."

"But I don't know where I am."

"You're in Bangkok."

"You know what I mean. You're supposed to take me back to where we started."

"What do you expect for half price?"

I decide to whine. "You wouldn't do this to a Thai girl."

130   "But a Thai girl does not ride through klongs with strangers for half price. Understand? Don't cry, just go up there and catch a bus. I'm going now, I have an appointment." He steps back into his boat.

I go up the stairs, cross the bridge and the street, and find nothing that even vaguely resembles a bus. "A bus?" says the street vendor frying noodles. "A bus, here?" I walk three blocks before I find a bus to take me back to Sukhumvit.

It's rush hour now. The bus is like a can of oysters, squished on all sides, oiled and salted with sweat. We clutch the overhead bars and try to plant our feet on the wooden floorboards. Slowly, I realize I feel sick. Sunstroke or food poisoning? Probably sunstroke. The Thai schoolboys in starched shirts stare at my wind-knotted hair, scorched face and general exhaustion. They look away and promptly begin discussing the ridiculousness of *falangs*, especially that one there, who is obviously hopeless. "I've been in the klongs today," I tell them in Thai, making sure to get the tones just right. They're surprised and embarrassed that I know their language. One of the boys—always there is a spokesman in these groups—looks me up and down, raises his eyebrows and asks, "Sunook, mai? Did you have a good time?"

"Yes, a wonderful time." I am attempting dignity.

"Did you go in a boat like other falangs or did you swim?"

"Very funny, very funny. I swam, you're right, all the way to Ayuthaya." Now they laugh. "Actually, I feel quite sick. . . ." and that's all it takes to get a seat, sympathy and two phone numbers.

April 10

THE YOUNG THAI MAN I first met in Chiang Mai actually lives and works in Bangkok. My brief bout with sunstroke is over and he is taking me out to dinner at a French restaurant. His name is Bom, pronounced quickly with a sharp high tone. Calling him is like calling a tropical bird, "Is BOM there please, squawk!?" He is twenty-six, very tall for a Thai, with the ancient, almond-shaped eyes and dark Indian features I've seen on temple walls.

131

The restaurant is romantic and air-conditioned. I wear perfume, Bom wears a suit. Still, it is hard to get poetry out of a man who designs bathrooms for American Standard, Inc. When I return from the powder room and gaze into his eyes over the red rose, he asks, "Were the toilets American Standard?" We have strange French food that must be good because it's so expensive, but really we are too nervous to notice. In Chiang Mai, we met each other a few times at parties, around other people, in nightclubs, with a lot of noise and dancing. Now we're surprised by how small the table is, how close we're sitting on either side of it. It's too quiet. We hear each other's teeth close on forks and spoons. We don't use the knives properly. I can't believe this has happened to me. I have no memory of blushing in Canada; now my face flushes apple red. I'm actually embarrassed to be sitting alone with a man. Thailand has turned me into a twelve-year-old again.

We cover up our loss of confidence by joking, laughing so hard the candle flames flicker. Bom tells me how the American men in his company say his name, leaving out the high tone. "Bomb, coman hava coffee. Bomb, whatcha doin' tommorrah? Wanna coman join us fer suppah?" He says, "It is so demoralizing to be called a bomb. I feel like a criminal." With all my usual delicacy, I point out a cockroach on the wall. "The menu lied," whispers my date. "This can't be an authentic French restaurant; the cockroaches in France can't possibly be that big."

After supper and a horrible Thai movie about a love affair between two people in an insane asylum, he takes me back to the Tylers' in a taxi. I click my teeth like castanets all the way there. "Why do you do that?" he asks. The taxi driver's eyes in the rear-view mirror brighten; he wants to know, too. "It means that—" I switch to English—"I want to kiss you." Only the darkness makes it possible to say such things. Bom is quiet for a moment. He looks out the window at the neon glare of the city, then turns back to me with a serious expression. "Is that what all Canadian girls do when they want to be kissed?"

He does not kiss me in the cab, because the driver, who is still staring back at us, would probably have an accident. He kisses me in the lobby of the apartment building, then immediately apologizes. "I cannot do this properly. I am too . . . shy." The lobby, he explains, is too open, too public a place for touching, even though it is after midnight and we are hidden behind two marble pillars and a grove of potted umbrella plants.

"That's all right." I am consoling and reasonable. I kiss him chastely on the cheek, smiling outwardly, inwardly urging him to scale the west side of the building with his bare hands to meet me on my bedroom balcony. No such thing happens. He holds my hand for a few seconds, snaps his teeth together, then goes away.

I run up six flights to the apartment and quietly change into my bathing suit, then go down to the swimming pool. I have to be held by something. I slide into the turquoise body of water and dance against my own rippling shadow.

April 11

I'VE BEEN A TYPICAL TOURIST here in Bangkok. I have shopped. And shopped. And shopped, mostly for shoes, as if I have a cancerous buying cell somehow connected to my feet. I am the second Imelda Marcos, and will end up giving away half the pairs I've bought. Bom heaves my backpack full of shoes through the riverside restaurant, trying not to knock anyone in the head or upset tables. I have my luggage with me because tonight I go back to Chiang Mai. "What's in here?" Bom asks repeatedly, unable to believe that shoes and clothes weigh so much. "Did you steal the Emerald Buddha? Do you have the Emerald Buddha in this backpack?"

The people in the restaurant stare at us as we work our

133

way around them. One of the waitresses who knows Bom quietly asks him who I am. "She is a half-Thai movie star," he whispers as loudly as possible. "She is very famous in Italy."

The waitress squints at me. "Aaah! It's true! I've seen her in a magazine!"

Bom pushes me on before I say anything. When we reach our table, he leans over to me. "Remember, to Thai people, all falangs look alike."

The backpack has such presence that we sit it up on a chair of its own and talk to it. "We will have oysters, prawns, calamari. . . . You," he addresses the pack, "will have plain rice and tea." I look at the menu, too, and pass up the serpent head's soup for the familiar won-ton. We eat and laugh, comfortable now that I'm leaving, pleasantly sad. If my Thai father found out I was sitting across from a good-looking man in a nice restaurant, toasting friendship and future lives (because of course in my next life I'll be Thai and marry Bom), he would be scandalized. That thought alone makes me happy right now.

Supper is over too quickly; we still have so much to talk about when we once again hoist the backpack through the restaurant, already rushing for the train. Bom hails a *tuk-tuk* and we screech through the traffic, reaching the train station with time to spare. Hooalampoong is the most tantalizing ugly place in Bangkok. Like any big train station, it wraps you in a vivid scarf of laughter, begging, crying. Flushed bodies sling the contents of lives from one place to another while train officials stride about with the air of palace guards. We manoeuvre around trucks, carts of battered suitcases and exhausted travellers. At the ticket booth, they tell us all first-class air-conditioned coaches are full. Second-class air-conditioned coaches are full. Second-class non-air-conditioned coaches with sleeping berths are also full.

I win a third-class ticket again; the gods are against me. I still have traces of heat rash from my last third-class journey. The ticket to Chiang Mai costs about seven dollars; I must not expect the Orient Express. Bom is very apologetic. "If we had arrived earlier, we might have been in time for a better ticket." We walk to platform five to await the train. I chirp, "Mai pen lai!" but he eyes me doubtfully. "Maybe you will travel with chickens."

"No, I doubt that very much. I've never seen chickens."

"I have, many times, in these trains, and piglets in crates."

"Well, what an adventure, then. Piglets!"

"And there are dirty old men."

"The young men are more dangerous."

A greasy fellow slinks past us, glancing over his shoulder at me. Bom grits his teeth. The little tendons in his jaw shift. "Mong bap jaa gin gnue-uh. They stare as if they were about to eat meat."

"Don't worry," I reassure him. "I'll be careful."

He sighs. The train lurches and belches up to the platform, settling into position. Bom loads my pack up into the coach. It's noticeably hotter inside the train than outside. Bom catches my arm when I move to sit down. "No, wait a moment." He produces a linen handkerchief and begins to wipe the seat. After some vigorous rubbing, he makes the mistake of examining his work. The cloth now carries a black imprint of his hand. We grimace. He's wearing beige linen trousers and a white shirt; though he says nothing, I know he doesn't want to sit down. We stand for a few minutes in the passageway of the train, saying various inadequate things. When the train shrieks its whistle and begins to rumble, we *wai* very formally and kiss quickly; I hardly feel his mouth touch mine. He turns a shade darker with embarrassment when a train vendor stares at us openly and chuckles. There is another ear-blasting series of whistles, a heave, and the train starts at the pace of an old man's shuffle. Bom hops down. I return to my seat and lean out the window. We don't say a word. He puts his hands in his pockets and looks down for a moment at his shoes, wrinkles his nose and looks up again. He grows smaller and smaller, becomes a white chalk-mark drawn over a colourful design. Distance slowly erases him and only the sprawling body of the train station remains.

The jungle of Bangkok falls, falls down, even the slums separate and scatter like shrapnel until there is nothing left but Thailand again, and her plain of green light. Men standing waist-deep in fish ponds haul in nets, their arms and chests like bronze mirrors. If the train were quiet, I would hear their voices.

April 17

THE SONGKRAN FESTIVAL is raging now in Chiang Mai. I arrive and have a bucket of water tossed at me. Pat comes dripping to the train station to meet me. She laughs, "This is crazy, I've never seen anything like it in my life. Crazy!" People pour ice water down each other's backs, turn hoses on neighbours, or drive around in trucks loaded with barrels of water. The city has gone mad with heat up until now, suffered the dry season with discipline. Now a three-day holiday of water slows everything to a wet standstill. Men dressed in business suits slip quickly across streets, keeping to the walls, alert for water snipers. Wet shoes squelch in houses and shops all over the city.

The parades, public parties, dances and drinking are ecstatic displays of kinship. People take foreigners home, feed, house and splash them, and send them on their way the next morning without remembering what country they were from. There is little difference between morning and night. Men and women line the streets and splash the crowd in the centre. Water balloons torpedo out of cars, soaking unsuspecting pedestrians. Pat and I wander around drenched, and we greet friendly strangers the same way they greet us: with a splash. Sometimes the water is flower-scented, mixed with talcum powder; people paint it on each other's faces and we roam around, white-striped natives reeking of jasmine.

At the end of the day, unable to stand the noise and press of the streets any longer, I go up to the hotel to complete my dosage of water by taking a swim. Before I dive in, one of the hotel attendants who knows me tosses a glass of ice water down my back.

April 30

MY RETURN TO DENCHAI is not a monumental occasion. When he sees me walking up Yantrakitkosol, backpack brimming treasure from the big city, Paw Sutape takes the cigarette out of his mouth and spits in the road. I greet him with "Sawatdee-ka" and a respectful if somewhat lopsided *wai*. He grunts, follows me into the shop and tells me, as I am climbing the first staircase, that the president of the Rotary Club—his brother—wants to see me immediately. Still unpacked and dirty from travelling, I set off again.

Denchai is asleep in mid-day heat, smaller and dustier, quieter after the excitement of Bangkok and Chiang Mai. I feel I've been away for months rather than a few weeks. The easy familiarity of the place is more comforting than I remembered. At the bridge, the river has shrunk to a trickle that murmurs a barely audible welcome. The *chong-nang* flowers growing up the steep banks are louder, and stretch upwards with purple and white mouths. Chickens and dogs are the same. They peck and pant in the dust with listless expressions. The worn faces of the shops are as familiar as grandparents. Merchants squint over their newspapers, then take off their reading glasses to greet me. "Aie, we thought you'd gone away." "Look, the glass bird has come back, the falang is here again." "Aah, Kalen! We thought you'd gone back to your country." "We thought you'd run away to Bangkok to marry a rich man." That last comment isn't a bad guess, but I explain I've just been travelling. They all offer me lunch, as is the custom, but I thank them and decline.

The welcome I receive from the president of the club is not so pleasant. Three other "fathers" are there, too, with grave faces. The Rotary Club is hurt, like an enormous five-year-old. I've been away for so long, I've forgotten Denchai, I've been whooping it up in the city like a wild foreigner, I don't have *greng jai*, that unique Thai quality which has no exact English translation. A person without *greng jai* doesn't know how to act properly. The word itself is used in a variety of ways. It means courtesy, respect, consideration; it is disgraceful to not have *greng jai*. Wrinkled foreheads accompany scowls and clicking tongues. I skulk out, feeling a strange mixture of indignation and guilt. Meh Dang leaps off the floor (she was chopping pineapple) when I wander dejectedly into the restaurant kitchen. She crows, "I thought you'd disappeared forever!" and throws her arms around me.

"But Meh Dang," I mumble into her shoulder, "I've only been gone three weeks."

"Three weeks is the beginning of forever!" she cries, always the dramatist, and drags me into the kitchen to listen to my adventures. As I tell her about the recent scolding I've received, a curious expression comes over her face. Setting down a bowl of ice-cream before me, she begins to giggle. "I knew this would happen. I mentioned it to Paw Teerug, you can ask him. Kalen, you had to expect it. You know women don't travel alone here, go away with suitcases for three weeks, it's not done."

"But I had their permission; they let me go."

She gives me a wry grin. "But what does that have to do with anything? Their permission does not change a custom."

Later in the day, Beed and Samat play Chinese checkers with me in consolation. "Hoo-a gow," they say of certain riled men. "They have old heads, they do not think in the new way. Do not worry about them. It will all blow over."

Beed's father shows me a new bird. I'm not my usual enthusiastic self. He laughs. "Aie, aie. So you really are worried, how silly. Don't you see? They are old men. You are a young woman. You don't have to be afraid of them. They are probably afraid of you! Mai pen lai!"

As usual, it ends with those three syllables. I go to Paw Prasit's for tea and watch him separating sapphires at his desk with tweezers like the forelegs of a silver insect. This effect is reinforced by the large magnifying glasses he wears—they make him look like a fly. He's the most Buddhist of all the Rotary members, calm as a cat in sunshine, and ever since that first day in Phitsanulok when the gibbons screamed at me, all he concerns himself with is my safety. "Ahh, Kalen, calm yourself. The other members of the club are not really so angry at you; they have been worried."

"But I phoned home, everyone knew where I was."

He pushes up his visor and rubs his sweaty eyes. "Yes, yes, but it is not the same as seeing you. Now you are here. We can hear your voice. We know you are safe. You smile. We know you are happy. That is the important thing. Come to the club dinner tonight and sing a song. Then everything will be fine." He chuckles, pulls his magnifying visor down again and returns to his table of gems.

May 2, 1987

OVER THE NEXT FEW DAYS I discover that several women have left Denchai for a couple of weeks—without their husbands. They've gone away to stay with their parents in distant cities, to visit working relatives or to return to the places where they were born. Though Dow and Older Sister Pla look after Paw Sutape, I'm sure Meh Somjit's absence has something to do with the general bad humour in the shop. She is in Bangkok. Paw's grunts are less expressive than usual.

Pla momentarily abandons her accounting chores to rush out and buy rice, fried vegetables and chicken from the restaurant next door. Without Meh Somjit and the small children here, we gobble down supper more quickly than usual and go our separate ways again. Pla is quiet for a Thai girl, very serious, probably the only regularly unhappy person I know here. On the weekends, we often go to talk with the monks—not about Buddhist theory, but about everyday problems. She does not like living with her relative, Paw Sutape. When she's not studying accounting in Prae, she works in the shop, even on the weekends, and he does not pay her enough—about forty dollars every month. She misses her family in Chiang Rai.

Dow, the regular accountant, only comes to visit Pla and help in the shop; she doesn't eat with us or help with the dishes as she used to. These last few days she is very quiet and often stares into the air, apparently studying the lazy movements of flies. Even more strange is the breathlessness that sometimes comes over her. She fans herself and splashes her face behind the house. Of course, there's a reason for this abnormal behaviour. In a week, she will marry Hoem, a relative of Paw Sutape's. He comes regularly for supper. I've met him several times, but there was never any indication that he and Dow were in love. Oh, wait—once he helped her take the dirty dishes away from the table and brought her a napkin. Other than that, I thought they hardly knew each other.

When Pla tells me about the wedding, I am doubtful. I see and talk to so many women here who are frustrated with their husbands but who possess that most feminine quality of smiling endurance. A teacher from Prae whose husband has another wife and child always says, "But I am happy because at least I do not live in Kampuchea."

May 4

LIKE ANYONE IN LOVE, I make excuses for Thailand's faults or I ignore them as much as possible. Meh Somjit is back from Bangkok, though, and she is continually pointing them out to me, highlighting the shortcomings particular to all small towns. She whispers her tirades while we chop vegetables behind the house. "How the people gossip in Denchai! It is so tiring. In Krung Thep, you can do as you please, no one cares if you wear black, if your skirt is a little above the knee, if you like to dance." Meh Somjit loves to dance, but Paw Sutape "says that sort of thing is for children and bad women." She squats, slicing cauliflower, looking up at me with eyes so wide and clear that I see my reflection. I am worried she's going to cut off a finger. "I miss Krung Thep.

I miss the streets, my family. I miss the klongs where my sister lives." Then we hear Paw Sutape's thongs smacking the floor, coming towards the kitchen door. "It is so hot, no?" Meh asks me. "But it'll start to rain soon, don't worry." His feet go away again.

She defends him. "He can't help being the way he is. He is from an old family. He is not so bad." She tries to convince me. "He does not jowchoo other women, like many husbands. I am his only wife. He loves his children."

I don't know the word for "ogre" in Thai. But Meh, you married an ogre, a troll! Even if I knew such words, I wouldn't say them. Her life is set down for her, a full plate. She has to finish it. Once Ajahn Champa said, "In Thailand, a woman rarely leaves her husband unless he is beating the children. That's about the only acceptable excuse there is." Now Meh Somjit pushes the vegetables away and fills a water basin, grabs the soap and begins—*sshhkk sshhkk sshhkk*—to wash shirts with a scrub-brush. I am a little surprised. Washing clothes is a morning chore and it is almost evening now. "Mai-yu-tay-tum," she whispers. *Sshhkk sshhkk sshhkk* against the washboard. "It's unjust." *Sshhkk sshhkk*. She shifts the fabric. White foam billows out of the basin. *Sshhkk sshhkk sshhkk*. She scrubs harder, undoubtedly scraping fibres out of the cloth. "Kwan!" she yells suddenly for her daughter, who is playing under the *chompoo* fruit trees in the courtyard. "Kwan! Come here!" The little girl appears, doll in hand, and stares down at her mother, who is soaked past the elbows with soapy water. Meh only glances up at the ten-year-old, whispers, "Fung dee-dee, Kwan. Listen well," then turns again to the scrubbing. For a few seconds, we hear nothing but *sshhkk sshhkk sshhkk*, ribbons of water slapping the pavement, Meh exhaling little pants on the downward strokes. Her hair pulls loose and falls in her eyes.

She stops, rests back on her haunches with her dripping arms stretched out over her knees. "Kalen, you are so lucky. You are so free. This is such a small place. Just the shop and the children and nothing outside. You can leave. You can do whatever you want. You don't know what you have." The three of us are very quiet.

Kwan glances from me to her mother to the soapy water. "Meh, ka?"

Meh is about to speak but Paw's feet warn us to change the subject. He has a nose for insurrection and worries when Meh spends too much time with me: I am white, barbaric, not to be trusted. I don't know my place. Now he calls her into the shop. Kwan and I sit alone in the courtyard, counting the bats. Only when the silver sky slides to deep violet do we go inside.

May 9

IN THE DAY'S EARLIEST HOURS, the women get up to continue the preparations for the wedding. Dow's face is glossed and powdered. For the first time in her life, her nails are painted, her hair is curled. Giggles and serious murmurs slip out from under Pla's door. By eight o'clock, the shop downstairs has been converted into a shrine of gifts, complete with pyramids of roasted chickens, ducks and oranges. It is thirty-two degrees when the wedding begins—our fine clothes are already damp. Over one hundred people form long lines in the street. We parade, shouting and singing, to Dow's house, where old Thai marriage officials will perform the rituals. People pack into the little wooden house—shoes crowding the staircase make it difficult to reach the porch. Inside, men stand around in solemn formality, dressed in suits they hate. Women glide about serving tea and *cow-tom*, rice soup, which the children try not to spill on their good clothes.

The ceremony begins almost in whispers. I can't really hear what is said between the old presiding couple and the young couple who are marrying. Dow and Hoem kneel on silk pillows before the old man and woman during the entire ceremony. Hoem slips gold bracelets on Dow's arms, gives her gold earrings and clips a gold braid around her neck. He is awkward and terribly serious. When the clasp of the necklace tangles in the wisps of hair drawn down on her neck, he blushes, embarrassed to be caught in front of so many people. His hands tremble. Dow is steady, black eyes almost unblinking, candy-red mouth very still. Her dress is the colour of a shell, pink verging on white, simple satin with a few lace frills. They give each other rings. The old Thai man and woman perform the rites and then place the cloth chain on the heads of the newlyweds, linking them. When they are finished, Dow and Hoem bow, rising half-way up in respect, keeping their heads bent before the old couple. Now they will go to the temple to receive a blessing for their marriage and to leave offerings at the shrine.

Everyone else descends to the garden to eat an elaborate breakfast and talk about the wedding. I don't tolerate parties very well, even Thai parties. The heat is exhausting, too; I'm already tired from rising twice in the night to shower. For a while I watch the fighting fish in the deep pool beside the house. Their ribboned tails are purple, blue and dark red. The children lean over with blades of grass and try to touch them. Always curious about particular names, I ask an older boy, "What are those called?" He looks at me incredulously. "Why, those are called 'fish'," he whispers.

"Meh Somjit," I bend down and murmur in her ear, "I have a terrible headache." She rolls her eyes and says, "I have one, too. Shall we go home?" A Thai wedding goes on from eight in the morning until two the next morning, with a brief break and change of clothes during the afternoon. Meh tells me she prefers *falang* weddings. "They're so much simpler, aren't they? Just the bride and groom down the aisle, then a little party, not all this shouting."

Two hours later, when I'm lying naked on my bed with the fan blowing hot air over me, I understand what she means. The shrieks of Thai girls fill my ears. They rise from the shop to the second floor before I realize they're heading my way. "The jowsow is coming, the jowsow is coming," they cry, feet beating up the wooden staircase. The bride is coming? Now? Yesterday Meh told me that Dow and Hoem would use my room for their nuptial eve because Hoem lives too far from Denchai to return to his home after the wedding. But she said nothing about their nuptial afternoon.

I still find this frustrating. In Thailand, I never know what will happen next, but everyone else does. I yank my dress on over my head, throw my dirty clothes in the closet, wipe off the dusty table with a stray sock, try to screw the tops on bottles of talcum powder and lotion. The girls are running around outside my door now, giggling hysterically. "Just a minute, just a minute," I yell, doing up the buttons of my dress and trying to find my shoes. When I open the door, Dow and Hoem are already on the stairs, with a small army behind them. The little girls string a gold chain across the threshold of the staircase. The bride and groom "break" through this barrier together. I hop out of my bedroom; the same thing is repeated at the doorway. As they enter my room, a great cheer bursts from the crowd of wedding guests. Paw Sutape actually yodels. It's not just yelling; it's yodelling. Thai men can yodel Swiss mountain-climbers under the table. They all start up this insane chorus of yodelling while the women put new sheets on the huge new bed.

It quickly becomes obvious that the sheets are too small. The women struggle and stretch, but a corner always springs off. The men slowly lose their enthusiasm for yodelling and put their suit jackets in a neat pile. We are all sweating now. I notice a pair of underwear hanging out of my closet and cringe with shame. The guests mill around the bed, or spill out of my room and chatter among the warehouse boxes of the third floor. Sparrows flutter at the windows. Dow and Hoem stand together rather sheepishly. Dow's lipstick still glitters, as if she hasn't opened her mouth since the paint was first applied. Hoem is sweating profusely and pulling at his collar, but he smiles now. How can a man be so earnest in the midst of Oriental yodels? Just when we begin to wonder if the sheets will rip in half from so much yanking, they finally remain in place. Everyone cheers and throws fresh rose petals on the bed, quilting it completely in scarlet. Then comes a shimmering downpour of coins to ensure the couple's prosperity. The men begin to hoot and cajole Dow and Hoem. The blushing newlyweds lie down together among flower petals and silver. They kiss each other once and very quickly, for the first and possibly last time in public. The wedding guests cheer. Finally, people begin to file out of the room and thump down the stairs.

Meh, Pla and the children go off to sleep. Paw continues celebrating with the other men and Johnny Walker. I spend the remainder of the afternoon sweating and watching a sentimental Thai movie, dazed with sleepiness and heat. I day-dream of Canada, where one side of the pillow is always cool and no one ever gets married in your bedroom.

IN THE EVENING after changing into even fancier clothes, we parade through Denchai to the open compound beside the market-place. The party has already begun, complete with musicians, eight Chinese dishes to choose from, and as much Meh Kong whisky as the men can drink. *Sunook sunook*—lots of fun—is beginning to tire me by this time; my smile is feigned. I don't understand why I'm here, sweating off make-up, listening to tinny music and laughing at bad jokes. I make the best of it and eat too many sautéed cashews. After the food, laughter and music drain away, the people begin to disappear. Dow has wilted and Hoem looks happy but anxious for sleep. The men want to dance now but their wives are too tired; children's arms loop around mothers' necks and do not let go. We're gorged on festivities, all of us, and want only to bathe and go to bed. It's almost two in the morning. Finally, the musicians pack up their vile guitars and synthesizers.

As I watch them, a boy crawls out from under the stage. At almost the same time, another one hops over the market fence and an older boy appears in the midst of the empty tables. He gives bags to the smaller boys and sends them in different directions. All three of them are kite children— children from the outskirts of the town, whose kites are made of newspaper. I know the oldest one because he sometimes works as a fare-collector on the *songtows* from Prae. He always wears a lopsided, oblivious smile. I watch as they tour all the tables, emptying half-eaten dishes, chicken bones and clumps of rice into their bags, drinking the left-over cola and orange soda out of the glasses, literally cleaning the table of scraps. Only once do the boy's eyes meet mine. He moves his head, becomes self-conscious, embarrassed; I smile but turn away before he does. There might be some dignity in not being watched.

May 13

SOMETIMES A GHOST OF RAIN comes down in the afternoons. The land cools off, sighs hot steam, falls asleep again. The heat doesn't slacken with these showers, but the ground stretches beneath them and begins to lose its dryness. I haven't seen steady rain for months—since I first came here. Logic, the curvature of the earth and the calendar begin to tell me terrible things. The cat who lives in the courtyard is pregnant again, her belly a globe of kittens. In my bedroom, I discover baby lizards who are too young to be properly terrified of me. I can pick them up without too much trouble. One of them is so small, pared to such a fine green wisp that I'm tempted to shut him in a book and dry him like a flower.

The seasons change carelessly. The new delicacies in the market are the great varieties of mangoes and sweet rices. Wasps are drowsy in bags of pineapple, licking licking licking the sweet yellow juice. I wander through the town, talking to

147

people I haven't seen during the last month. Time never moved so quickly until I came to live here.

May 17

TODAY, AS ALWAYS at six o'clock, the national anthem blares into the streets from the police station. Obedient to custom, everyone driving and walking stops and stands at attention. I, however, am pedalling Meh Dang's old bicycle, which has no brakes. I whiz by three or four cars, humming "Lucy in the Sky with Diamonds," before I realize what time it is. Dropping my feet to the ground, I drag myself to a stop in front of the station. Four officers on the terrace lean over the rails and laugh.

I continue to make these cultural blunders through sheer absent-mindedness. The other day, coming home from Prae, I dropped a few coins and reacted as a *falang* would when a quarter begins to roll across the floor: I put my foot out to step on it. But such a reaction is not Thai. In Thailand, the money carries the sacred image of King Bhumibol. One doesn't stamp a lowly foot on the king's head. As soon as I bent down to pick up the five-baht piece, the discussion in the *songtow* died. I slapped myself mentally, retrieved the coin, expressed an apology to the king's image by holding the piece between my hands and bowing. An older Thai farmer snickered aloud. These *falangs*, I heard him think, what *barbarians*.

May 22

SCHOOL BEGINS AGAIN and the return to a routine of study is more welcome than I expected. It's good to be back at Nareerat with Ajahn Champa, Peroontip, Yupa, Glanjanaa.

My Thai reading teacher, Sangkaya, has brought me a new book to work on. I can actually read the language now, slowly, faultily, like a very small child. The students are the same as always, excited about the beginning of the new year, not yet complaining about homework. Everyone brims with stories of summer; an energetic pulse of gossip beats in the air.

I have a full schedule of new classes this term, and one of them is quite beyond me: law. There are too many formal, abstract words whose tones I can never reproduce properly. There are confusing historical precedents I know nothing about, having been unable to take the class last year because of the inferior level of my Thai. It's a difficult, tiring class, and there's no way I can read the accompanying texts. The only reason I attend it is for the teacher.

I don't even know his real name—it's too long to pronounce. In class we simply call him Ajahn. The other girls have nicknamed him The Tiger because he has an eye-toothed ivory grin. He's very dark, a southern Thai, and wears suits from Bangkok. He's tall for a Thai man. To emphasize certain points, he raises his left eyebrow or snaps his fingers. "He is too . . . charismatic," hisses Ajahn Champa. "Too flashy." The old white eagle—our headmistress—resents his lack of respect for formality and his daring ideas. I don't know much about his ideas, but he tells a great joke, walking back and forth in front of the blackboard with glinting teeth. The men who unload the rice sacks across the street from Meh Dang's might be his brothers. Those men do not wear linen suits; they swing hooks into sackcloth and heave the heavy bags down with naked arms and backs. After speeding down the highway on the tops of their loads, they arrive in town wind-blown, wide awake, black eyes snapping. The Tiger has the same fierce features, but he knows more about historical precedents.

He's considered unattractive by most of the teachers. "He is much too dark," says Peroontip, who is admired by all for her own pale complexion. Glanjanaa, who has grown hugely pregnant during the summer, murmurs, "He is a wolf. I would not ride in the same car with him." Sangkaya clears her throat. "Who would marry a man like that? His skin is black, he is too bony, and he has that ugly scar." A long time ago, The Tiger almost lost an eye; a scar hooks the outer edge of his eyelashes to the lower part of his cheekbone. Yupa, the youngest teacher under Ajahn Champa's direction, snaps shut a dictionary and stands up. She speaks in excited English. "I have found it! I have found the word for The Tiger. P-I-R-A-T-E. How do you pronounce?"

"Pirate."

"Pirate." She tries it out. "Pirate. Yes, that is the perfect word." She returns the dictionary to its place, then whirls around, dramatically taking hold of my arm. Yupa should have been an actress. Fluttering her eyelashes, she begins in an earnest voice, "My dear, I don't think you should take him back to Canada with you. They would not let him into the country. He looks like a PIRATE! Oh! The sadness!" The other teachers clap and chortle.

I pull my arm away from Yupa, laughing. "Of course they would let him into the country." I pause. "But who said I wanted to take him to Canada, anyway?"

"Aaah!" Peroontip giggles, speaks in Thai. "Kalen has fallen in the hole of love." I clear my throat, roll my eyes and rush off to class, leaving my Thai teachers cooing behind me.

He is not at all a pirate; he just has . . . presence. Pirates don't wear Paco Rabanne aftershave. Unfortunately, most of the students agree with the teachers (big-bellied Siphon says he is a smiling demon), but even if they don't find him attractive, they still can't look him in the eye. If he stands within two feet of a girl when he's asking a question, she blushes deeply, begins to giggle, and ends by hiding her face in a nest of fingers and papers. Unfortunately, he has almost the same effect on me and, because I'm so white, my blushing is even worse than a Thai girl's. If he corners me with a question I can't answer or asks me for a comment I don't have,

I almost melt with shame. I know, I know, I am regressing. For the first time since I was eleven years old, I have a crush. I fantasize about my law teacher. It's so humiliating.

May 26

I RIDE OUT INTO THE FIELDS on Meh Dang's rickety bicycle, hoping the tires will endure the wagon ruts and puddles. Already the wheels groan with effort. I'm about an hour away from Denchai, pleasantly lost in the clay maze of country tracks. If people knew I come out here regularly, they would start tying me up. Meh Somjit thinks I'm at the monastery with Ajahn Ramyong. It's strange enough to sit alone in my room reading a book, but to be alone in the fields is unthinkable. I pedal past scattered farmhouses and groves of fruit trees. My shins are coated with the same red dust that rises behind the bicycle.

Silence flows into the shallow valley, disrupted only by my passage. When I ride through a small hamlet of houses, everyone is motionless save three children. People snooze in hammocks strung between trees and truck bumpers; they doze on benches and wooden divans and woven mats. Only children have the energy to move. When a small boy sees me, he squints, opens his mouth and nudges his sister. I pedal closer and closer. He stares in wonder, as if witnessing a mirage. "Who is it?" he asks his sister.

"It's a falang!"

"A falang!"

As I pass, I hear the older sister say, "It's a girl." They're silent until I'm farther down the road but then their laughter follows me. Once I'm out of the cluster of farmhouses, I take up counting again. After twenty, I started losing track of the dead snakes; now I'm only doing scorpions, toads and frogs. Seven black crushed scorpions, six squished toads, two dead frogs and one living one. There are too many water buffalo to count. They almost vanish in mudholes, submerging their great bulk and remaining invisible until I'm beside them. Only their long horns give them away. They are such pacifists, these animals, so Buddhist, so Thai. I rattle by and they do not even raise their heads. They meditate as they chew their cuds.

Today the mountains are dark blue, but clearer than they've been all season, each swell, canyon and cliff cleanly etched. If I pedalled hard for five minutes, I might reach the valley's edge and stand at the foot of one of those blue giants. The sky is no longer the spiritless plain it was during the dry season, but again a deep ocean. I am in sunlight; then, within a breath, a weightless sail of shadow covers me, my eyes dull and a cloud washes over. I pedal faster and the sky shifts. Sunlight splashes me in the face again, startling my eyes. This race with the clouds happens again and again until I'm dizzy. I grow exhausted from chasing sunlight.

Half-way across a drained rice paddy, an old woman talks happily with her cows. She has enormous buckets on her shoulder-poles. Seeing each other at about the same time, we simultaneously raise our hands in greeting. She puts down her buckets and comes slowly across the stubbly field. I drag my feet on the ground. "Where are you going?" she asks. "What are you doing out here?" She is surprised to see me.

"Looking around." I look down the road, up the road. She laughs. Two hump-backed tawny cows walk up and nudge her hips. She pushes them away.

"Aren't you afraid?" she asks.

"Of what, the cows?"

"No, no, daughter, not the cows." Again she pushes one of her nosy friends away. "Come with me to the house. I will give you some water and oranges." I leave the bicycle at the rice paddy and walk back with her to a grove of trees. Hidden inside is a small community of old houses and broken-fenced corrals. At the old woman's home, I wait beneath the house while she patters above me. Three little boys in the nearby trees are shooting mangoes down with slingshots. They're each about six years old, knobby-kneed, missing front teeth. "My grandsons," the woman announces when she appears again with water and oranges. The mothers of the boys come out of their houses to meet me. A young woman shows off her small baby, holding him up in the air, singing to him. We sit in the shade beneath the house, talking of Canada, rice harvests and ice. One of the boys can't believe it's possible to walk across a whole lake in the winter. "But how does the water get so hard?" he asks, knocking his knuckles against the floor.

When they speak among themselves, they use the northern dialect. I lose half the words in the singsong dips and curves of the language. The boys' mothers bring *som-tam* and a warm basket of sticky rice. We spend the rest of the afternoon eating, talking and singing. The boys show me a game similar to jacks, but which uses stones and coins instead. It's always humbling to play games with children who have the dexterity of brain surgeons. I don't know who is who, which child belongs to which woman, which woman is an older sister or an aunt or second cousin of the other. The children call every woman "mother" and every woman calls the other women "sister." The grandmother invites me into the loft of the house to show me the rice baskets. After threshing the rice from its stalks in the field, they store it in enormous boat-like baskets. The surplus is bagged and sold in the markets of Denchai and Prae.

The house smells of lemons and mandarins. The old woman, her daughter, her son-in-law and their children live in the two simple wooden rooms, each with a mat-like bed and a few shelves. The cooking and washing are done on a large open-air porch which has mango trees for walls. "We have picked all the mangoes we could reach," says the woman. I could be in a treehouse.

When it starts to rain, I'm invited to stay and nap until the shower passes, but I explain that my family in Denchai is expecting me. We patter down the steps. One of the boys runs off to fetch my bicycle. The baby is sound asleep, so we whisper our goodbyes and I thank them again for lunch. As I pedal out on a small road, the boys run behind me, racing each other. From a distance, I stop and stare back at the tree-eclipsed houses. The last child on the road waves and trots away. I try to memorize the place; it's so small from here, dwarfed by the surrounding expanse of sky and land, its lives hidden in leaves. A storm billows above the tree grove, shadowing the country with a purplish scroll of clouds.

When I turn again to the road and flip over the pedals to begin my ride back, I see another snake, fine as satin piping, sliding between the two wheels of the bicycle. If I moved my foot, my toes would touch him. I stop breathing. Let him slide up through the spokes—I want to take him home! He is perfect, green as a tendril in sunlight, tapered at the tail. As he passes under me, I slowly lay down the bicycle and follow him. He does not move—he is pulled, drawn, sipped across the road like liquid through a straw. At the first small bush he rises, rises, defying gravity, delicate skull floating up to the narrow branches. The light rain seeps through to my skin as I watch him.

He is all the grace I've ever seen, a slow vein of emerald. When he meets the twig he's been waiting for, he cleaves onto it and slides into the cross-hatched branches. I squint, lose focus for three seconds—but not once do I look up, or away—and the snake is gone. I can't believe it. I draw back branches, peering inside. I walk around the plant and bend over to examine the underside of the twigs. I soak myself searching for a metre-long reptile who has simply vanished. For a long time I stare at the bush, awed as Moses, but nothing happens. The snake has turned into wood and leaf. I hop on the bicycle, hair plastered to my forehead. I will never forget that disappearing trick, that artless plying into thin air. I splash roughly through puddles now, mindless, my brain wound up with miraculous green ribbon.

154

May 28

I WALK ALONG YANTRAK in the early evening, hands in my pockets. Near the train station I meet a German man drinking Singha and waiting for his train. He speaks no English but manages with a rolling Bavarian Thai. The local policemen come into the little bar to listen to two foreigners slipping and stumbling through their language. The German has lived in Thailand for six years; he has a Thai wife. He loves it here, but he can never find any shoes big enough to fit him, and he misses good bread and strong cheese. "But the beer is great," he assures me. "Cheers."

I wonder about foreigners, myself included. Some of them live here because they cannot live anywhere else. The German is friendly but embarrassing. He rampages with his voice; he stands up to make a point. His clothes are from some other decade and his eyes have a peculiar sheen. He has the happy-go-lucky charm of a well-fed tramp, though he tells me he is not a tramp. He is the director of a wallet-making company. He tells me his wife is "like a sun." The Thai cops nudge each other and chuckle. The German is indignant. "Thai men are terrible for having women on the side, but I'm not like that. It's a great country for a man, but let me tell you, it's hell for a woman."

The cops chuckle again. They repeat the Thai proverb about the hind legs of an elephant. "I love my wife, but she will always do the washing. Men weren't made for that sort of work," one of them says. He takes out a horseshoe-shaped pipe and snorts some grey powder up his nose, then coughs and shivers. "It's simpler if the wife just has babies and helps her husband. Everyone in North America gets divorced." He shoots me a triumphant glance.

"You see?" says the German. "They don't even think about equality. It's so sad." He undoes some of his buttons, does them up, drains his beer. We hear the train whistle. "I have to go buy my ticket," he says reluctantly. We stand and shake hands—the policemen mutter. Shaking hands is a graceless farewell gesture in the eyes of many Thais. They prefer the smooth movement of the *wai*. The German stumbles across the road, grinding gravel with his too-tight shoes, waves and disappears into the station.

I wander to the bridge. The new flow of water in the river has swept back the algae. A fresh shade of green coats the trees and tangled riverside plants. I walk to the monastery, but Ajahn Ramyong is not there. Instead of turning back, I keep going. The monastery is on the edge of the fields and it's already getting dark, but I know the nearby roads quite well. A chalk-mark of moon lights the sky. When the town is behind me I begin to run, for no particular reason except to feel the hardness of the road. I could lope all night, to Burma or Vietnam, listening to snakes and insects, frogs, my feet beating the ground. I leap over puddles and flattened toads, pass people in wagons so closely that I almost touch the ribs of their water buffalo. The sun collapses in a red blaze on the tops of the mountains.

I run until darkness kindles starlight, until the fields are pearled black plains flickering farm-lights and small farms. I am drenched with stars. "The origin of all life is starlight," I remember, then think of something Ajahn Champa told me the other day. "If you look at the moon upside down, you will see the shadow of a hopping rabbit." I stop, bend over—and laugh out loud. There it is, a silver-grey rabbit leaping in the night sky. Running back into the town, I turn around a dozen times to thank the moon.

June 4, 1987

I FIRST HEAR THE MUSIC twanging and banging out of the general hoopla of the market-place. It is morning; the people are quick-footed. As I come closer, picking my way through parked bicycles and motorcycles, I hear a tambourine accompanied by the steady boom of a drum. Expecting a small band of children, I find instead a gnarled old man sitting on the ground between the coconut milk pastries and the pineapple cart. He is tuning a handmade instrument and setting up a battery-run amplifier.

This is the latest travelling musician in Denchai. He is missing one eye, has a cataract in the other and cannot walk without crutches. His left foot is a mangled knob of flesh and his clothes are cleverly situated rags. His voice is magnificent. He has spirit. He is a one-man band, not a beggar. His instrument is made of a large, empty oil tin (the drum), two catgut strings running up a neck of wood, and a tambourine attached to the top of this same neck: a very primitive cello with a circus tambourine. Sitting on the ground with the cello between his legs, he draws his bow across the strings and thumps the oil can with his good foot. His mangled foot, though useless for walking, is still capable of movement: a string runs from the tambourine to his big toe, and by wriggling his crippled leg, the tambourine rattles.

But it's his voice that astounds everyone at the market. He doesn't sing beautifully, doesn't warble like a fairytale bird. No, he sings like two cats in an alley; it's impossible to know if this explosion springs from violence or love. For the first five minutes, his voice is a perfectly tuned wail accompanied by twangs and rattles, a lament with an oil can. What inspires awe is the power, the range of the sound, because it comes from so tattered a body. The people in the very back of the markets look up to see what's happening. Someone dropped an old pebble into Denchai and a mountain erupted. He bangs and shakes and beats away, crying all the while, sawing furiously at the strings of the cello.

I stand and tap my foot, staring at this wonderful old man and his tortured oil can. I'll never see such invention in Canada. A small crowd gathers; someone requests a song. The requested tune is much more open and light, not a wail at all. The clink of coins in his dish is regular and encouraging, and the people clap and laugh when he plays a song they know. The market women gather and ask for more. A young boy brings the musician a pitcher of water and one of the fruit-sellers sets her umbrella behind him, taking the sun from his head. We listen until the old man finally wraps up his instruments, scrambles up with his crutch and hobbles behind the market.

Later, in the deep hours of the afternoon when the light is very sharp and people drowse and gossip after lunch, I see him on the steps of the train station, slumped in the shadows, dreaming. His dreams are like dogs' dreams of chase. He twitches without ceasing. The hands in his lap still play, plucking away, rising, falling, fingers wide awake; the crippled foot still jerks down on the tambourine cord and the good foot thumps at the oil can, though the instrument itself is set against the train station wall, draped with old cloth. He plays in his sleep. Only his voice is missing. I stand in the white light of the dusty street, waiting for him to break into a ragged song, but he remains quiet. For a long time I watch him dream. I'm afraid I'll wake him by staring so hard, but his sleep is stronger than my eyes. When I have seared his image into my memory, I turn away and walk home.

June 9

AFTER A DAY OF LIGHT that blinds more deeply than any darkness, the sky turns. The wind drags over the hills and thunderheads roil up, wave after wave of heavy blue cotton. First the curtains leach at the screens, then explode upward when the wind exhales through the house. I have not felt such wind since I first came here. I rush all about the house, whispering, "Let it rain, let it rain!" I remember the drumbeat that forced us to shout to each other in the badminton court. I remember the green I first saw here—I would become a horse just to taste that colour.

Now I stand on the back balcony to watch the season's first lightning. Shutters slam all down the streets, people close up shop, pedlars gather up their goods and hobble away. Umbrellas in the market blow down and shouts fly up with the pigeons. Children giggle for no reason. Red chickens flap in a squawk under the houses, as though swept by a giant invisible broom. Soon Meh will scream up to me from the second floor and I will rush down to help her collect the drying laundry. It's going to rain, finally, and it's going to rain hard. I can even hear pigs from the slaughterhouse snorting their excitement. The lizard on the outside kitchen wall cries *tu-kae, tu-kae, tu-kae*. Frogs, birds and crickets compete with the wind in an out-of-tune chorus of chirrups, squawks and cooing.

Lightning bursts behind the mushrooming clouds. I stand and wait for the shocks, trying to imprint them on my

159

mind because they could never be captured in photographs. Light heaves, rushes, cracks down and disappears; the wind beats me wide awake on all sides. The sky opens like an enormous mouth and roars.

June 13

PAW SUTAPE IS AWAY in Bangkok; the house breathes easily. Meh Somjit, Pla and I laugh, eat *som-tam* and sticky rice, watch Chinese operas and discuss the best-looking actors. The children run through the house and play hide-and-go-seek up in the warehouse. I am even allowed to go with Meh Dang and Maw Piya to a small village outside the province. Maw Piya has patients there.

The houses of the village are set far back in the trees. It's dusk; the smell of earth blends with that of steaming rice. The doctor has brought us along for company, and tells Meh Dang she doesn't need to come to the house to help him. We stay outside together, walking towards the fields, giggling when we trip on tree roots. When we reach the edge of the woods, we stand quietly, listening to bits of murmured conversation and the rattle of plates in the village houses. The air smells like a god's salad. We stand with our heads up like horses, noses awake. Suddenly Meh Dang lets out a cry. "Do you see? Look, look at them!" She points to a little footbridge barely visible in the half-darkness. Lights wink above the shallow stream; for a moment I think people with cigarettes are standing on the bridge. I squint. "What is it?"

Meh Dang laughs. "Hinghoi! Insects of light." I see fireflies for the first time. The two of us run after the flickers of light. Meh Dang catches one first. She calls me, opens her hand and we lean over to watch the light blink on and off. I put a finger on the light, expecting it to be warm; the spark lifts into the air. Meh Dang and I almost bang our heads together.

For the rest of the evening I catch fireflies, want fireflies as pets, want to raise a colony of fireflies and have them flitting in my room, sparking down on my shoulders. It gets darker and darker, and Maw Piya comes out of the farm-house to find both Meh Dang and I trotting around like goats. We finish with a bagful of fireflies, but the doctor says, "You are both quite crazy. Let those creatures go."

And we do. Meh Dang shakes out the bag, scattering light, and I flush them all into the trees. She says, "I want a part that glows. I want a light." Before we get into the truck, Meh Dang turns to bow to the woods. We laugh. She talks all the way home, telling stories of insects, frogs kept in bathrooms to eat the mosquitoes, a cobra her great-uncle used to love, the indubitable aphrodisiac power of reptile intestines. Her voice shines into us all the way back to Denchai.

June 17

LIN, DEN, BOH AND I go out to the fields early in the morning, play tag on the motorcycles and race to the river. We even startle water buffalo with our singing. We go from road to rough track to grass and thorn an almost invisible path. The water is smooth in the morning. The sky is rippled silver and fog still curls in the valley. We strip to our bathing suits and slide down the mud into the water.

The sandy riverbed makes me want to ask about leeches, but I don't know how to say "leech" in Thai. "Are there any worms that suck blood in this water?" I ask.

Boh and Deh turn around and stare at me, horrified. "Do you have them in Canada?"

"Well, yes, sometimes. They usually live in this kind of place." Both boys scream and stick their feet into the air, treading water with their arms. Lin asks how big they are, and after my explanation both boys relax again. Deh thought they would be the size of snakes, turtles, alligators.

We spend the morning in the water, then go to the closest village for a meal of fried vegetables and *guitio*. With dust in our hair and mud on our legs, we have chopstick fights for each other's noodles and water. The woman in the grass-thatched noodle-stand gives us free Coca-Cola for helping her unload rice sacks from her wagon.

On the way home, we sing at the top of our lungs the currently popular song "We Are the World." Deh makes the ride as bumpy as possible, racing Boh, revving the bike like a fine-boned Hell's Angel. We fly back to Denchai, covered in mud, with bugs in our eyes and faces dry as leather masks. When Meh Somjit sees me, she asks, "Have you been in a war?" She threatens to hose me down in the courtyard if I don't bathe immediately. I rush up the stairs, humming. I have lived a perfect day.

June 23

AFTER MANY PHONE CALLS across the country and the regular grilling by my Rotary fathers, I get permission to travel alone to Bangkok to meet Goong Samakeemavin. We find each other in the station immediately after I cut my finger on the metal siding of the train door. It's now bleeding profusely and Goong has to find me a handkerchief before he can hug me. Goong is a young Thai man who stayed with my family in Canada for six weeks in the spring. I've talked to him several times on the phone, arranging this trip, and to meet him now is like greeting a childhood friend. Many of my mother's letters spoke of him, the Thai son, and I was so anxious to come to Bangkok that even the snorts of Paw Sutape couldn't stop me. After my finger is well wrapped, Goong says, "I thought you would be much taller." He glances down at my finger. "Aie, we must wash that or it will get infected." We climb into a taxi, both of us talking at once. Goong brings a tangible slice of Canada with him; he talks of my brothers and sisters as I would, about my mother, the dog, the unpredictable Canadian weather.

"Do you want to see the photographs now or later?" he asks, pulling out a thick envelope. My mother has sent me very few photos during the year, and I am anxious to see these. The first one is astounding. I hardly recognize my sister. She's no longer a scrawny tomboy. She's been transformed into a long-haired female wearing lip gloss. Only a year, and this has happened. My younger brother looks strange. "What did he do to his face?" I wonder. Goong squints at the photo. "Aaan, his . . . his . . . how do you say?" He puts his hand to his forehead and suddenly remembers the word. "Eyebrow! That was the week he shaved off his eyebrows."

"What?" My brother is twelve years old.

"He shaved off his eyebrows because a boy at school said they would grow back in half an hour."

"Are you serious?"

"Yes, really. He was very disappointed when they didn't grow back." We both peer down at the photo again. My brother resembles a little troll.

When we arrive at Soi Pradu, I'm surprised. Because Goong has been overseas and speaks English, I assumed he came from a wealthy, stylish family. Soi Pradu gives me a different impression. It's a narrow twisting street jammed with noodle carts and motorcycles and honking *tuk-tuk*s. The house where he lives is three storeys of Chinese newspapers, old bird cages, boxes of books, kites, clothes, all coated in dust and presided over by a yappy terrier cross furry rat. Presently, she's tied up in the kitchen; every time she strains at her rope, plates and tin cups clatter over the cement floor. Goong explains, "You see, it is disorganized because we are moving house. My parents are working all the time. My grandma is in the hospital. My brother is at school. The only one to clean up was my grandma. That's why the dog barks. It misses Grandma. Poor dog." He leans over to pet the terrier, and also flicks a big cockroach back into the kitchen area. "They usually stay in the kitchen and the bathroom," he says. "Maybe they're just coming out to meet you." He looks up with a grin, notes the expression on my face and says, "Just kidding."

After showing me my room and helping me make the bed, he suddenly remembers my finger. Down in the kitchen, I complain the iodine will sting, but with redneck Canadian gusto, Goong says, "Don't be a wimp, man. This is Thailand. Everything gets infected." A few roach antennae twitch in glee and Goong douses my finger.

June 26

LIFE IN THIS CHICKEN COOP with Goong and his brother Gop (*goong* means shrimp, *gop* means frog) is very entertaining. His parents are already in the new apartment, so we have Soi Pradu all to ourselves. We are irreverent, happy and very loud together, discussing all manner of things, principally sex, which we must discuss in English because I know none of the Thai words for it. Goong is the first Thai to teach me any taboo vocabulary. During the day—if Goong goes to school—I go to Wat Prat Gaew and other temples to wander around dazzled by the murals, statues, walls of glass and intricate gardens. If Goong skips his classes, we go swimming or to a museum or to a coffeehouse where we eat ice-cream in air-conditioned luxury.

Because he knows my family so well, we talk about them again and again. I feel an awful twinge of Canadian reality. Today I booked my return flight for August 19, two days short of a year. Impossible. I feel I've always lived here. Time has taken on mysterious proportions. I don't remember Canada as I did before: it's a great distance from me, even in my mind. When I stumble through my mental landscape of the city, I greet a few people, yes, my family, three close friends, then I trip into the hole left by Michael. That is why

164

I dread going back. Though I don't feel it now, I'll feel his absence when I return.

Thinking of that is tedious; I ignore it as much as possible. I try to live entirely in Thailand now, learning and touching everything I can in the short time I have left here. I have trouble sleeping for the restlessness of my mind. I cannot close my eyes for fear I'll miss something. When we swim in the day, Goong tells me to relax. Nothing is chasing me.

At night we go dancing with his friends, run the circuit of castle-like discotheques where young people gather in throngs to drink and sing. Bangkok nightclubs entertain a great cross-section of people, everyone from Thai teenagers to famous actors and actresses to drug-dealing thugs. The younger people swaying back and forth and singing the Thai songs word for word make a fascinating contrast to the completely different crowd of Americanized Thais, who are very sexy, very aware of being watched. Public displays of passion rarely take place, though. Even the society people still maintain Thai modesty. Foreigners with astonishing pale eyes and flushed white skin are less traditional. Overweight tourists paste themselves to the perfect bodies of the prostitutes.

The dancing people twist together under the lights. Their clothes and skin are drenched in perfumed sweat. Voices spiral around me, seemingly unattached to mouths; I wonder where Goong is hiding. He is undoubtedly after the Italian girl whose curly mane of dark blonde hair constantly tumbles over her green eyes. "But her breasts are much too large," Goong has complained, explaining he likes the smaller, firmer breasts of Thai women. Apparently, a big bust is her only fault, for she even speaks Thai quite well. When I finally find Goong (the Italian beauty is nowhere in sight), he scolds me in English. "Where have *you* been?" to which I retort, "Me? Where's the blonde bombshell?"

Goong's voice trails off. "What is bombshell?"

"Mai pen lai," I shout over the music, "it's not important."

When we return to Soi Pradu, the narrow street is asleep

and empty at last. The cockroaches retreat when Goong turns on the naked lightbulb and begins to make tea. Exhausted and happy, we talk in low voices while peeling our oranges. The terrier snores. Goong becomes nostalgic about Canada, my eyebrowless brother, my mother; she also sat up and talked with him late at night. After a long silence of tearing apart orange peels—the whole room smells of citrus—Goong exclaims, "When I return to Canada, I will marry your little sister." I laugh. We are both afflicted with the same disease. For us, countries live in people.

July 1, 1987

TONIGHT WE GO TO THE HOSPITAL to visit Goong's grand-mother. Hospitals in Bangkok are real hospitals, antiseptic and haunting, a terrain of ghosts in oxygen tents. Silent nurses glide in soft shoes: no slapping thongs around here. We speak in whispers. Goong's parents have welcomed me into their family like an only daughter. In the critical ward with them, I bow my greetings to Grandmother. She is a flaccid yellow skin of the woman Goong described to me, the tireless worker, the one who ran stairs instead of walking them. She is in her nineties and slowly drowning in the fluid of her lungs. Her family gathers around her, holds her hands, whispers to her. She smiles and fades in and out of coherence.

Goong and I slip out of the ward because he has a wreath of jasmine to offer to the Buddha. But instead we come to an impressive statue of the Virgin Mary, her face predictably benevolent, a slight smile curling her mouth. The hospital is Catholic. Her arms are held out in a gesture of welcome or in the first motion of embracing. Goong offers the Virgin his wreath of flowers by looping it around her wrist, then closes his eyes and prays in the Christian way. I am silent and respectful during this act of worship, but when we are walking back, I say, "I thought you were Buddhist. We left offerings the other day at the temple."

"Yes."

"But you just prayed to the Virgin Mary."

"Kalen, if it is going to help my grandmother, ease her suffering in any way, I will worship them both. I was educated in a Catholic school. I am a baptized Catholic. But of course I am a Buddhist. How can I not be a Buddhist? It is in my blood, my history. The gods don't need names. Only men need names."

July 8

IN THE EARLY MORNING in front of the Erawan temple, dancing girls come dressed in silk and woven gold. Worshippers whose wishes have been granted send the dancers here to thank the gods, who are fond of dance. They arrive before the roar of traffic begins. Goong and I go to watch them and help feed the monks in the nearby monastery. The monks arrive barefoot, eyes downcast, the silence of morning wrapped about them as gracefully as their saffron robes. We place bags of rice and the choicest oranges in their alms bowls. A whole group of laymen lines up on either side of the walkway, each with a sack of food for the monks. When our supply dwindles and the monks have made their rounds, we return to the shrine to watch the last of the dancers. Like the monks, their grace is timeless, pulled inward: they are performing for an invisible public. Their hands twist through the still air, pliable as warmed copper. When they finish, they bow to the ground three times, then float away. Scattered rose petals paint the dark ground red. After the girls go, the temple yard is motionless. Goong and I bow to the old Buddha. The jaws of Bangkok are beginning to open, but only in a yawn. Sunlight draws a crimson curtain over the walls of the city;

Goong and I watch the flaming scape of clouds. We've hardly spoken since we left the house this morning.

When we have both risen away from the shrine, a strange thing happens. A woman with red hair and pale skin walks behind us in bare feet. She wears loose black trousers, a worn green blouse and a red mask in the old Commedia style. The fierce arched eyebrows and hooked nose create a grand miserly expression. Goong and I just stare at this bizarre apparition. She seems intent on speaking with the Buddha. First she bows and mimes an introduction with him, taking off an invisible hat and shaking his hand. She talks to him with her hands, leans forward, listens to some whispered instructions, nods. Then she leaps like a lunatic in our direction. Goong and I involuntarily step backwards.

She dances the way Scrooge would dance, all bones and sharp movements. But unlike Scrooge, she begins to pull coins out of the air, from under rocks, from behind the branches of a small ornamental tree, piling them in the centre of the compound. She approaches Goong and I, bows and enthusiastically shakes my hand, as any *falang* would. She takes both my hands in hers, opens them, then spreads her own hands, which are large, thick-wristed and empty. For a moment, we stare into each other's eyes. Hers are green, surprising in a land of black-eyed women. When I look down again, there is a fifty-baht bill in my palm. She dances over to the little collection box, scooping up her small pile of coins on the way, indicating that I should follow her. She deposits her coins, discusses something in mime with the Buddha and looks back at me. I have not yet moved. She points to the collection box, the Buddha and the fifty-baht bill. Meanwhile, Goong is rummaging through his pockets. "I had fifty baht. I had fifty baht." The dancer rubs her fingers together and points to the box again. I walk over and slip the bill in. For the first time, she makes a human sound. She laughs.

A group of young monks and visitors to the shrine has gathered now. They, too, stare with surprised faces at this new dance for the gods. One of the monks goes away hurriedly, his face solemn. The masked woman continues to spin and spring over the ground. The people watching her smile and laugh at her discussions with the Buddha. Within minutes, an abbot from the monastery appears, but when he sees what's happening, he chuckles and nods. She plays the crowd like a marionette gone mad. She pretends to hoard up their money in a leather pouch, then, realizing the Buddha is right behind her, she is obliged to surrender the coins to the box. "Ha! Ha!" Goong whispers. "Did you see that? She keeps the bills! Did you see?" But if she does keep the bills, no one else seems to notice. The crowd has grown; people are taking out their cameras and snapping pictures. I try to get a glimpse of those eyes again, but she is busy hooking other people with them.

Finally, exhausted, sweat dripping down her neck and darkening her back, she bows to the crowd. We clap for her. She turns and bows deeply to the Buddha, who smiles. Then she walks away. She heads straight for the street, still barefoot and masked, but relaxed now, walking with a loose spine. Goong and I look at each other, start speaking simultaneously and then laugh.

I suggest we go and talk with her, find out where she's from, how long she's been here. We walk out to the street, but the traffic has started up and she's already on the other side. We missed the light. Her mask is off now, and she must have had her knapsack hidden away somewhere, because she's now pulling open the top. She takes out a pair of black sandals and slips them on. When the light turns and Goong and I begin to walk across the street, she hails a *tuk-tuk* and leans over to argue prices with the driver. I call out to her, "Falang!" but she doesn't hear me. The *tuk-tuk* pulls away from the curb into the traffic. She disappears. I joke with Goong, "Who was that masked man?"

He shoots me a funny look. "Kalen, that was a woman. And she was very crazy."

July 10

THAT CRAZINESS is the nature of Bangkok. It's one reason why I love this filthy city. It is wild, unpredictable, and does not answer the questions its own streets create. All day long, whenever we wander through markets and crowded lanes, I scan the faces for a red hook-nosed mask, but I don't see her again. That's asking for too great a coincidence in a city of eight million people. When Goong and his parents take me to the train station, I expect her to leap off one of the trains in a black cape, but unfortunately, my departure is very calm.

A first-class seat waits for me and I have plenty of time to buy some snacks for the day's journey. Goong's parents have come to make sure everything is in order. We take a series of grinning family portraits together, disturbing a snoozing train inspector to do the final big picture. Goong's parents chat with the older couple next to me. They're visibly relieved to know I'll be supervised until I arrive in Denchai. The old couple owns a small umbrella factory in Chiang Mai. Goong's father tells me to be very careful of strangers. His mother, who is a big, practical, Chinese businesswoman, says, "She's a big girl. She's not stupid. She'll be fine." Goong and I say our goodbyes in English. We hug each other, making the old couple strain their eyes. "So I'll see you before you go back to Canada, right?" Goong asks.

"Of course. Maybe I'll come and stay with you before I leave."

"Yes, that's a good idea. Yes, that's what you should do. I'll show you the rest of Bangkok and we'll go dancing again and my friend Rodney will be so happy. He's madly in love of you."

"With you," I correct him.

"Right, with you."

The whistle blows and Goong's father sticks his head in the coach. "Hurry up. You want to go live in Denchai?" We laugh. Goong gives me another hug, then hops out of the train.

Again I am leaving. The city drops away as I stare through the smoked glass windows, thinking I prefer third class because you can lean out into the wind, breathing up the smell of whatever is around you. I wish I had more time for everything. This is the way my life will be, then: a blown mural of moments, people, places, none of them solid. The land closest to me slips by in a blur.

I feel the city of angels spread inside me: I think of the narrow lanes, markets, enormous buildings, people, people, people, Goong, his friends and family. I feel the earth as I rush over this country, and I am sad. The day is not long enough, the night is shadowed with sleep. It is July already. It is late. I am in the midst of everything now, and none of it can be held tight enough. I think of the masked green-eyed girl who danced through the temple yard, belonged to no one, and disappeared into the day like an unknown character leaving a dream. Where is she now?

July 11

I HAVE RETURNED to a small, private tragedy. Meh Dang's most trusted servant has been discovered stealing from the cash box of the shop. Meh Dang is in a sad, resigned rage. Paw Teerug is in Bangkok, which makes everything much worse. The servant, Gnop, is hiding upstairs, too ashamed to show her face, and a terrible heaviness weights the air of Meh Dang's house. It seems as though the fans are broken and the cross-wind which so often cools the house has died. Sak and his friends from the badminton court skulk in and skulk out, strangely quiet. Meh Dang sits at a table with paper and pen, scribbling out furious little black slashes. She is trying to figure out how much Gnop has stolen. "I cannot believe this! Thousands! Do you know why? She doesn't even keep the money! She sends it to her boyfriend in the army! So he can buy liquor, cigarettes and those cheap little prostitutes at Pattaya. Fool! Ahh! This is so bad. I have looked after her. I have cared for her, fed her, brought her away from a dirty hut in Chiang Mai. She sleeps in the same room as my children. We eat together. And she steals my money! I cannot believe it!"

I have never seen Meh Dang in such a broken state. The people can smell the bad feelings; no one comes into the shop to eat. Even children with coins for ice-cream melt away when they see Meh Dang's closed-up face. She tells me the shop has been losing money every month, there are so many bills to pay, the children have to go to school, Paw Teerug has been away for so long, she is so tired, so tired.

Gnop's small baby begins to wail. Though he is upstairs, his screams slide down the banister and echo off the high ceiling of the kitchen. Meh Dang's face contorts. "Aaah! I will go mad. That child is always screaming, always. I have such a headache." The baby's shrieks rain down on us with such constancy that I wonder if he's been hurt. When I rise, Meh Dang pulls me back down, saying, "No, nothing's wrong. He cries like that every day."

She rubs her brown forehead and moans, "Where is Paw Teerug?" I'm unable to say anything to comfort her. I give her a massage, waiting for each pocket of muscle to lose its hardness. I bring her some cold tea. The baby stops crying. She pushes away the scraps of scribbled paper and puts her head down on her arms. For the first time, I see the shop as it is when it's empty and sad. The glasses don't match. The tables are plywood covered with plastic. The walls are dirty, coloured by posters of fruit and ice-cream and beautiful, kitten-faced women. The floor is chronically dirty. Flies lick up the left-over juices from the bowls of departed customers. Tawny dogs stick their muzzles in the garbage baskets outside. Meh Dang pulls her head up from her arms and picks up one of the glasses on the table. "Do you see this? A glass. Glasses crack. If you can see the crack, the glass is broken, it is of no use. It must be thrown away."

The baby begins to shriek again. Meh Dang arches her long neck and stares at the ceiling. "That is not my baby. Why has she done this?" She leans the full weight of her head on her hand. "I miss Paw Teerug, Kalen." The gnawed pencil scratches at the paper again. We say nothing more until I go home. She gets up to start supper, crumpling the calculations as she rises. "I think I will go to Chiang Rai soon," she says. "To see my mother and sisters. I am so tired of this place." Her eyes survey the shop and then wander out to the road where women from the sawmill are riding past on their antique bicycles.

Before leaving, I take hold of her hand for a moment. She smiles, then turns back into the shop. As I walk away, I hear her call Gnop to come down and help prepare the evening meal.

July 14

STRANGE, THAT I STILL WAKE in the morning sometimes and am surprised to be here. I'm roused from sleep by a truck-load of acrobats. No one is sure where they came from, or when. Meh says they were already here at dawn, singing and beating their one huge drum, warming up in the field near the train station. Apparently, they materialized out of the morning mist, seven of them in various shapes and sizes, dressed in tattered pink and green costumes. After breakfast, I walk down Yantrak towards all the noise, prepared to follow them around.

The market is bustling with people and the acrobats are ready to perform. They are an odd but splendid collection—a flock of chickens with peacocks' plumes—all young boys making a great deal of gleeful noise. It begins at the train station: two beat out a galloping rhythm on the big drum, singing an unintelligible song while the other five perform a variety of stunts. The smallest boy must be eight years old.

He scrambles up the bodies of the four older boys who already stand on each other's shoulders, forming an unsteady column of arms and legs. Several times I close my eyes, afraid for the small ascending acrobat. He's so like a monkey that I expect to see a tail and watch him swing into one of the teak trees.

On top of the highest boy's shoulders, he lets out a shrill whoop and the crowd—for there is a crowd—cheers and claps and leaves bills in the dish balanced between the ears of a mammoth Chinese dancing dragon lying motionless in the dust, waiting to come alive. The tower of acrobats teeters as the boy scrambles down the stairs of knees, shoulders, heads. Once on the ground, he takes a charming bow, smiles, flips over backwards and bows again. He is thoroughly enjoying himself. He is a ham. With a snap of the wrist, he takes up the silver dish and slips his brown length through the crowd, grinning broadly and making sure he gets money from everyone with eyes. "Anyone who sees us has to pay," he informs me and rattles the dish. "Come on. Falangs are rich." He looks up at me with a businessman's pragmatic smile. His teeth are rounded and large, lined up in smooth, tight rows like kernels of ivory corn. Unlike most Thai children, his face is thin and long, making him look older than he actually is. He rubs his big toe in the dirt and grins. "Come on, Older Sister."

"But I'm not rich, you know. I'm not a falang. I'm a half-Italian Thai nun." I show him the Buddhist charm around my neck. "See?" He is city-born and bred, nothing like the gullible children of Nareerat. He laughs, does a Rumpelstiltskin dance, shakes the dish and trots away with my money.

From the train station they roll and thunder to the liquor store, where Pee-Moi and Meh and the boys greet them like long-lost relatives, though Pee-Moi says she's never seen them before. "They must be a new group and, oh, how long it's been since acrobats have come to Denchai!" The boys pair off and start juggling empty bottles of Sang Som whisky in the air. They juggle while springing up and down the steps, spinning around, touching their big toes to their elbows, clapping in time to the drum and cymbal. When they stop, not a whisky bottle broken, two run back to the field to get the dragon.

Once the dragon rises, the children of Denchai flood the street in an enthusiastic wave. After looting the liquor store—Pee-Moi is outrageously generous to street performers—the incorrigible beast twists up Yantrak towards the market. Only the smallest acrobat and the drum-beater are visible now; the others are deep in the innards of the silk-backed dragon. He barges into every shop along the way, the jeweller's, the drugstore, the duck and goose restaurant, thrusting his pink- and green-feathered face over the counters. The boy runs up with the silver dish, announcing that a performance will take place near the market in half an hour. Whoever is behind the counter is delighted; a dragon swaying over your morning paper and bowl of rice soup is a good omen. The drumbeats boom through the street like a giant's footsteps, and people lean out their windows to see who's coming.

The beast swings his tail when children try to catch his tassels and streamers. I've never heard such breathless laughter. They can't get enough of this spiral-eyed devil whose head is bigger than an elephant's, whose feet are made of simple sandals and toes. They race the heaving monster and scream when he suddenly lashes out at them. He twists, roaring up one side of Yantrak, then down the other. Meanwhile, the little acrobat shouts news about the grand finale at the market-place, and collects money for an event as yet unseen. The drum-beater, tired from pushing his instrument around on a metal carriage, shakes sweat out of his hair. Nearing the market-place, the dragon roars his loudest (hidden acrobats smell fried chicken, coconut sweets, roasted bananas) and flies high into the air. The boys emerge with sweaty faces, blinking in the sudden sunlight, and the performance begins.

People from the market come out to see what's happening. Again the swaying tower is formed, toes clutching shoulders, hands gripping feet. They are tired now, groaning from the bottom upwards. The crowd gasps when two different acrobats lose their balance, half slipping from slick shoulders of the boys beneath them. When they are finally balanced, the little gibbon flies up, his fingers and feet digging into his fellows. Some of them grimace and blink salt out of their eyes, but the little one grins, unworried about the pain his sharp-boned feet inflict. At the top, he turns around, balancing one foot on the boy's head while switching the other to his opposite shoulder. Everyone stares upward. The children are awestruck; wide open mouths reveal a few gold fillings.

The boy loves this. He reaches into a pocket, lights a match and tosses a few firecrackers over our heads. The explosions scare the dogs and make us jump simultaneously as if we've all hiccoughed on cue. A boy beside me grabs his jaw and groans: he's bitten his tongue. The top acrobat turns around again with a fearless chuckle. Reluctant to give up this high main stage, he bows a few more times. The crowd cheers when he finally begins his descent.

Once disassembled, the boys flip through the air, casual gymnasts in old pyjamas. Their stained costumes have holey knees and ragged seams. Two pairs set to juggling anything the crowd will give them: a bottle of fish sauce, a child's toy, a Chinese turnip, a mango, a crab. One of the older boys turns away from the group and takes a long drink from a flask. He slips into the middle of the street where one of his companions holds a lit taper in the air. He then blows out his swollen cheeks, breathing a huge flame towards the crowd. Its heat licks our faces; some people draw back, gasping, which makes the smallest acrobat shriek with pleasure and hop up and down. The troupe likes this part of the show the best. Their eyes gleam in admiration as the fire-breather tips the bottle of fluid, fills up his cheeks, then blows it into flame again. Children screech and cover their eyes. Men shake their heads with wonder, women with horror. I suddenly sneeze, nose itchy from gasoline fumes.

The dragon rests, enormous and tangled, on the ground. In my mind, the fire-breather becomes that creature with swirled eyes. He is ferocious enough to be a dragon, grinning maniacally as orange tongues leap from his mouth and curl to black wisps. There should be more evidence left behind from this performance, something should be burning: the temple, for example, or the old teak hotel. At any moment, Siamese soldiers on elephants should come charging from the tennis court.

The last flame is a transparent ribbon. The fire-breather coughs, spits and rinses out his mouth with water. His red face streams sweat; his shirt sticks to his back and chest. The money-collector slips into the crowd. When the audience has been well picked, the acrobats bow and clap, thanking us for filling up their dish. The crowd, in turn, applauds them one last time before slowly dispersing and returning to morning business. The troupe goes to buy food in the market.

The youngest acrobat guards the dragon, who's been abandoned in the street by everyone but children. The boy tells them to be careful, not to be rough, to calm their hearts if they actually want to *touch* it. The children become solemn. They slip their hands between the monster's jaws, squealing as quietly as possible. A girl smaller than the dragon's head kneels before it and reaches up to trace the pattern of its eyes. Then other children do the same, stretching out pale-palmed hands to stroke the rainbow pupil. When the other acrobats come bounding out of the market-place, they drop the dragon down over their bodies and begin to howl, driving the boys and girls away in a fit of ecstatic shrieks.

At the train station, the boys load the food, the drum and the dragon into the back of a very rusted-out truck.

Observing my sceptical eye on the vehicle, one of the boys says, "We call him the Brown Turtle." He jumps up into the box, untangles silk, feathers and tassels, then wraps the dragon's sleek body around its chin. The troupe is on its way to a small village outside Prae where one of them has a sister. "She has a place to bathe," adds the fire-breather, who is sucking on a piece of ice. Three of them get into the cab of the truck and the other four sit in the back, slurping orange soda out of plastic bags. We agree they must come to Canada as soon as possible; they'll look for me when they get there. After they roar off up Yantrak Road, I'm left standing in a haze of red dust near the train station, smiling so hard my face is sore.

July 17

THE RAIN IS NOT the insistent droning force I expected it to be. In fact, the weather has changed so gradually and naturally that I barely notice how much it rains. Showers end quickly and the sun tumbles out of white cloud castles. We step gingerly over the puddles like cats, shaking mud from our feet. It often pours at night; we wake to wet roads and an even greener sheath covering the earth. Plants grow so quickly that I make myself stop and watch the visible unfurling of tendrils and leaves.

When I show too much interest in what happens in the dirt, my friends make fun of me. Today, Lin leans over and whispers, "Do those little trees speak English or Thai?" I laugh.

"Kalen, have you ever seen mai-yer-rap?"

"Is it a plant or a meal?"

"A plant!" She takes my hand and leads me to the field near the train station, a place I often visit alone. At a certain point along the path, she stops and flings her arms open above a patch of dark weeds spotted with pink flowers. I am not very impressed. "Look closely," she says. I squint at the plants and she picks up a few pebbles. "Watch." She leans over the shrubs and sprinkles the stones like cinnamon.

The small leaflets close up, stung by the rain of rocks. The movement has the smooth symmetry of a fan closing, or the slats of a green blind pulling shut. Lin takes a long stick and sweeps it over the dark emerald carpet: the colour disappears, leaving behind dark curled weeds. An involuntary gasp comes out of my mouth. Lin squats, grasps her knees and giggles, pleased with her surprise. "So there is no mai-yer-rap in Canada."

"I've never seen any." We crouch on the edge of the path, waiting for the plants to forget us, to slowly open again, stretch their fingers away from the dark stems. I think of the gentle, cautious movements of sea anemones. I run my thumb along the edges of a long row of leaflets and they fold quickly, sensitive to touch.

We walk back towards the liquor store so I can visit with my first family. Prasert is in Prae, so Pee-Moi and I scurry to the kitchen. Lin stays out at the stone table and reads the newspaper. Deep inside the house, the air is thick with the smell of rice and spices. Meh has just finished frying chicken, and the old German shepherd is whining. Pee-Moi throws her the glistening innards, then turns to me. "I want to go to Phitsanulok, like my sister, and get a regular job in an office." She spends all her time running the shop, doing the accounting. "My eyes are already getting bad. I will get old." She washes her hands, then starts on the pile of plates, talking more to herself than to me. "But then there are the boys and the grandparents. Someone has to help, Meh can't do everything by herself. How could I leave them?" Very easily. Many Thai women who feel trapped know what is wrong; they even have the ability to free themselves. But most of them do not have the raw courage and necessary selfishness to break with convention. In Thailand, history is not a subject. It is a force that holds you still. Pee-Moi is twenty-eight, soon to be considered an old maid because she has no boyfriend.

Many of my letters home are written in self-righteous rages after listening to the women here tell me their woes. They are everywhere: I live with them, they teach me at Nareerat, they sell me pineapples, they chat with me in the backs of *songtows*, describing their abusive husbands, their husbands with two wives, their husbands who disappear for days and days on business trips. After these confidences, they cautiously add, "But don't tell anyone." I am white and constantly stirring things up, talking about women in North America. "No," I tell them, "it's not true that everyone in the West gets divorced and has crazy children! Look at me!" And I make a hideous face to prove my stability. Today, I haven't the energy for outbursts because the air is too muggy and sweet. I listen to Pee-Moi because she needs someone to listen to her and she knows she can trust me, but I won't go off on any tirades about being strong and taking control of one's own life. Saying such things is a waste of breath. And today, I have spent long hours with Lin; her brash good spirits always make me regard everything with a completely Thai outlook. I only have to spend an hour with her to believe that the wisdom of *mai pen lai* is unquestionable. Ajahn Champa says I should be careful or I will end up married to a Thai man myself, washing clothes by hand and forgetting my English.

Lin goes home at about five, leaving me to spend the early evening with Pee-Moi, Meh, the boys and the grandparents. After supper, we watch cartoons. As usual, the grandparents laugh more than anyone else, adjusting their glasses after particularly hilarious scenes and sucking noisily on camphor candies. Though they are both near ninety, it's clear that death is the furthest thing from their minds. Koon Tah still climbs up on the roof to repair the drainpipes after heavy rains. The boys and I sit on the floor in front of the television, eating peanuts. Geway makes a show of doing his English homework, but really I'm just pointing out the right answers to him during the commercials.

181

When Jaree, the servant, comes home from taking a liquor shipment to Prae, the boys both run up to meet him. His rough-knuckled hands are closed in the shape of a shell. "I have something," he announces, which makes the boys paw and jump at him. "Just a minute, just a minute. Kalen, come here for a second." He opens his hands. A black beetle takes up a large portion of his left palm. Its snout curves outward into two large horns, the upper one extending past the lower one. A rhinocerous beetle, the size of an egg. I've seen them in books. This one is completely still. Jaree assures me it's dead. Though the boys are jumping around, begging him to give them the bug, he asks me to touch it first. I lay a fingertip on the armoured back. It's smooth, harder than an insect should be, and cool as a stone. "Press harder."

The beetle is not dead. It hisses, expelling the air from under its shell, and starts marching over Jaree's hand. I put my hands beneath his and it falls into my palm. The children laugh when I shriek. They can't believe that large insects still raise the hair on my neck. The beetle seems even larger than before, now that it's crawling towards the pale flesh on the inside of my arm, gripping my skin with its claws. It's *holding* onto me. I turn my arm and feel it pinch me. This makes me nervous. I try to shake it off. It won't let go. I put the fingers of my other hand around it, tug and fling it away. Jaree says, "No, no, no," as I realize that, in trying to hold on, the beetle is tearing away clawfuls of my skin. My arm spots up blood.

"Why did you pull him away? He wasn't going to hurt you. You scared of those horns? They don't move, Kalen." The hurled beetle struggles on its back, legs swimming in the air. Jaree picks it up again and puts it in Geway's hand. The horns, he explains, are to scare other creatures away. "They worked perfectly." He laughs. Rhinocerous beetles are harmless vegetarians. The boys put it in a basket with a peeled banana. Geway turns to me. "Haven't you ever seen one of these before?" He holds up the basket where the beetle is already gnawing at the fruit.

"No, I haven't. They don't live in Canada."

He nods gravely, as though my deprived childhood in Canada—no rhinocerous beetles!—disturbs him. "Could you take this one home?" He brightens, offering me this gift.

"I'd like to, but I don't think he would enjoy the airplane ride. Thank you very much though." For the rest of the evening, we play with the beetle or watch him working on the banana. I'm surprised to learn such a bulky creature can fly: when the children toss it towards me, the rhino takes wing with a loud drone and barrels forward like a miniature airplane rapidly losing altitude. It crashes on my shoulder with a graceless thud. I scream. Jaree wonders if the beetle will find its way to my room by morning; large insects with horns are naturally attracted to *falangs*. Pee-Moi tell me not to worry as she coaxes the creature off my neck. After the children have gone to bed, she'll let the beetle go in the garden.

July 21

TODAY IN THE TEACHER'S staff room, Sangkaya, Glanjanaa, Yupa, Peroontip and I had a huge feast of *som-tam* and chicken salad. Ajahn Champa doesn't like me to spend too much time with the teachers, but they are my best friends here in Nareerat. And Ajahn Champa is at a conference in Chiang Mai. The English department is relaxed; teachers take off their shoes and sit cross-legged at their desks. Yupa went to the cafeteria and bought the *som-tam*; Peroontip made the chicken salad here in the staff room.

We stuff the papaya salad into our mouths with sticky rice, our faces flushed because of the peppers. We have just discussed some curious English words and now we are talking about sex. These conversations are always coy and hilarious. Glanjanaa is extremely pregnant, soft-spoken and beautiful. Her eyes *melt* into other people's eyes. She makes you think that being so pregnant in such hot, humid weather is comfortable, even relaxing. As she leans over her belly, a secretive, mysterious expression transforms her face. "Kalen, may I please ask a question?" I nod. She lowers her voice even more. "What is . . . wooing?"

I lean towards her, just as serious. "Wooing is what you do when you want someone to fall in love with you."

"So what do you do?"

"Glanjanaa, I think you already know."

"But how is it done in the West?"

"The same as it's done here, I think, but faster."

"Yes, but what do you *do*?"

"All kinds of things. You go out to movies and dinners and dances. You give flowers, chocolates, little gifts. You write love letters. You know."

She nods thoughtfully. "I don't know." She smiles. "I wonder if men in Canada woo better than Thai men."

"Canadian men are great kissers." I finish off the last of the *som-tam* and dry my fingers on a handful of pink napkins.

Glanjanaa looks at me with raised eyebrows. "Where do they kiss?"

"Where what?"

"Where do they kiss?"

I get up, lean over her shoulder, glance around for effect and whisper in her ear, "Ev-er-y-where!" She bursts out laughing. Sangkaya, Yupa and Peroontip are anxious to hear what we're talking about. As this bit of conversation works around the room, teachers twitter in mock horror and ask comparative questions about Thai and Canadian men. Sangkaya, who is happily married and has a baby daughter, sighs heavily. "It is a pity I was not born in Canada," she says, fanning herself.

Yupa, the only unmarried teacher in the English department, has a serious question. "Why is 'nake' not a word?"

"Pardon me?"

"Nake. Why is it not a word, in the present tense? Why is there only just naked?"

"Because naked is an adjective, and nake just doesn't exist."

"So nake is not a word, but naked is, and so is nude?"

"That's right."

"So what is the more sexy, naked or nude?"

"But Yupa, they are the same thing."

"But I mean the word, which of the words is the more sexy? Would you say, 'I saw a beautiful naked man in my bedroom' or 'I saw a beautiful nude man'? Which is more pleasing?" By this time, Yupa is blushing Indian red; the other teachers are laughing into their hands.

"I would use 'naked' myself."

"One more question. We can make 'sweet' into a verb by adding 'en'. Sweeten. But why can we not say 'colden'? As in, 'I want to colden the water.' " Everyone listens for my answer.

"Yupa, the word 'colden' just doesn't exist in English."

"Yes, but why not?"

"Yupa! I don't know!"

"You want to be a writer, no? Should you not know these things, Kalen?"

A smile weaves into the lines around her mouth and eyes. She is teasing me. I deepen my voice. "English is a very great mysterious language, Yupa, like God." She laughs, rolls her eyes and we start eating the chicken salad.

July 25

EARLY IN THE MORNING, before school, Meh Dang's son Sak appears at the shop and whistles for me. I am in the kitchen scrounging for something to eat. (For reasons unknown to me, a great deal of food always disappears overnight, and I often eat breakfast at school.) Sak is hopping up and down at the open door, motioning for me to come talk to him. "Meh Dang wants to see you before you go to school, it's very important, she has a surprise for you." I slip on my thongs and disappear before Paw Sutape gets up and asks me where I'm going.

I find Meh Dang wide awake, singing in the kitchen with blood and chicken innards laced around her fingers. When she sees me, her mouth slips from song to speech like a bird coming down. "Kalen, sawatdee, how are you today? Never mind, I know you are fine, you are always smiling, I have a surprise for you." She looks up from her chicken to see if I'm listening to her rapid words, then grabs another naked chicken and cracks it open. "I want you to come to Chiang Rai with me, okay? I talk to Ajahn Champa, I talk to the Rotary Club, they let you come with me, of course."

I am doubtful. "Meh Dang, you know that Paw Sutape will say it's too dangerous. If I can't go to Prae with you in the evenings, he isn't going to let me go to Chiang Rai."

Meh Dang is taken aback. "Dangerous? Dangerous? With Meh Dang? I look after you like my own daughter! Dangerous . . . ," she scoffs. "Chiang Rai is the best city in Thailand. I was born there." Here she smiles self-indulgently and tosses chicken guts into the bucket at her side. She stands up to wash her hands. "All this permission business. What could possibly happen? You need permission from the club, from all your fathers here in Denchai. It's very boring. Do you need permission from Mr. Prem to go pee?" Mr. Prem is the prime minister of the country. She glances into the shop, looking for eavesdropping spies, and whispers, "Did you know that Paw Sutape is not really Thai?"

"He's not?"

"Of course not. He's a monster from Laos!" She covers her mouth in terror, then her eyes.

We both start giggling, but I say, "Meh Dang! How bad!" On the scale of prejudiced Thai insults, you can't get any lower than calling someone a monster from Laos.

Now she begins to hack away at pineapple with a butcher knife; the muscles in her arms tighten all the way into her neck, shifting beneath her skin when she changes position.

186

"Do you want to eat some of this? It's very good, you know." Without waiting for a response, she gives me a large sweet slice. "I will give you a dozen pineapples if you come to Chiang Rai with me."

"Meh Dang, I *want* to come, but—"

"I know, I know, it's too dangerous. Oh, Thailand is bad. The men are big strong children who never wash clothes. Not good at all. Always asking if we can go somewhere by ourselves. In Canada, it's not like that, is it?"

"No, it's better in Canada."

"Wait a second! Now it's better in Canada. I thought you loved Thailand! Lies! Lies! You want to go back to the land of ice!"

"Meh Dang! I meant the men! And I don't want to go back. But weren't we talking about Chiang Rai?"

"Yes. We are talking about Chiang Rai. You're coming with me because I don't want to go alone."

"I really don't think Paw Sutape will let me go."

Meh Dang just laughs at this, pineapple juice on her lips. She has no qualms about talking with her mouth full. "Kalen, what a surprise. You will come, don't worry. I am Meh Dang, you know."

July 28

WE ARE ON THE FILTHIEST BUS I've ever seen in Thailand, which is quite a remarkable superlative. It is the common bus, the Orange Crush, without air-conditioning, reliable brakes or comfortable seats. It is crammed with people—crying children, greasy-haired men, tired market women carrying loads of fruit and corn. In the back, a small crate holding four violent chickens wobbles back and forth. Every few minutes, they try to peck each other to death, then subside into strange gurgling threats.

"The best way to do this is to sleep all the way to Chiang Rai. Hold onto your bag until we get there, okay, Kalen?"

"How long will it take to get there, Meh Dang?"

"Not long. If we had a car to drive, maybe four hours."

"But how long by bus, Meh Dang?"

"By bus? This bus?"

"Yes, this bus. How long?"

"Oh, six hours or so. I'm not exactly sure. Just take a long nap!"

Like many Thais, her talent for sleeping is extraordinary. It doesn't matter that she is sitting up on a wooden seat: within an hour she falls asleep. I can't keep my eyes closed. The farther north we go, the more awake I become. The land spreads out in pleats and waves. Cross-hatched fields roll towards terraced hillsides where women stand ankle-deep in water, planting rice. The sky blows down mist and rain.

July 29

WE ARE STAYING in an old teak house with Surapong, the lawyer who used to live in Denchai. This morning I lean over my mattress to squint between the floor planks. Blue flowers and lime green moss grow ten feet beneath the house. The man next door keeps three monkeys in a large wire cage; his yard is crowded with mango trees. I wake up with the monkeys, whose cackles serenade us through breakfast. Surapong has already gone to work, leaving Meh Dang and me his car for the day.

"But don't ever tell Paw Teerug about this," she cautions me as we get in and unfold a few maps. "Forget the maps," she says when we find them too confusing. "We will go to Maysalong without maps. I have not been there for many years, but am I so old? I will remember the way."

Maysalong is the high mountain in the Golden Triangle. During the communist revolution in China, many people escaped across the border into southeast Asia. Some of the villagers came here after travelling the long journey along the spine of mountains between Laos and Burma. The Thai government allowed them Maysalong as a refuge and they have been there ever since, living on the mountain as Chinese people would, speaking their own dialect of Chinese and adhering to Chinese customs.

We are already deep in the hills on roads that switchback higher and higher into mist. The mountains walk green out of the clouds; we travel an arm's length from the sky. Meh Dang tells me a few horror stories about crazy communist hilltribes, murderous Laotian soldiers, gold thieves, drug smugglers. Her fingers on the steering wheel make spidery gestures. "It's not safe up here, you know, not safe at all." She flashes a grin in my direction. "Want to go back? Never can tell what those madmen will do with a pair of weak women, especially one with white skin."

"Meh Dang!"

She hoots. "I am kidding!" Though the stories are, for the most part, true, Maysalong is not deep enough inside the Triangle for us to encounter any trouble. I hope. I've read chilling newspaper articles about groups of tourists being held for days without food while communist bands from Laos decided what to do with them. Such articles do not always end happily.

We are, as they say, in the middle of nowhere. Meh Dang has grown strangely quiet and pale. When I ask her if she's all right, she whispers, "My stomach says no." Each time we round a curve, the road behind us disappears. Only when we climb a new ridge can I look down to see where we've been. The terraces of rice cannot stand these angles; they slip backward into the valley, leaving the land to the rougher green of bamboo groves, banyan trees, leathery, razor-edged plants. Even the people are different here, darker skinned beneath simple clothes, often barefoot, walking solitary up the centre of the steep roads. When the car passes, they stand off to one side and stare at us.

This place is too high, too hard. The mountains heave and

plunge at random. The land holds itself but nothing else. I can't believe people live here. Even the road cracks and narrows, devoured by the earth. This is a cliffside over the world, a new country inside the one I thought I knew, a wilder place than I was prepared for. I expected something like the hills that surround Chiang Mai, but a different feeling exists here. Far below us, like the sun-licked land in a fairytale, the valley of Chiang Rai shimmers in a sea of silver-threaded green.

On the road above us, I glimpse a man walking with a shaggy pony. The pony is very small, rust-coloured, and carries a load of wood on its back. When we switchback up to the old man, he does not move away from the car until I can see the vertebrae buttoned down his naked back. I wonder, then, if he is so old. The man is a skeleton painted brown. He smiles when he sees us and his skin pulls tight over sharp cheekbones. His ribs are two ladders rising towards his throat.

Meh Dang whispers, "Ah, you see? You see, over there? That is Maysalong." Four ridges away, a mountain littered with brown huts and brick buildings rises out of the green roughness. Before we get there, Meh Dang stops the car and barely yanks back the hand-brake before leaping out. For two minutes she coughs and heaves at the side of the road. I hand her some tissue and the water bottle when she is finished. When she hops back in the car, she is smiling. "I feel much better now."

The village of Maysalong is a brown clump of roots grasping at the mountain, barely anchored. What do they do in storm winds? When we drive up the road into the village, we see a few bicycles and battered trucks outside the unpainted houses, but nothing moves. It's begun to rain, but the roads were already wet. Red earth swirls with grey mud. The people, mostly old men hovering in doorways and windows, have exhausted eyes. A small group of children stares at us silently. Their feet are caked with mud.

We drive through the town to the plateau of the mountain

where the Chinese run a market, a restaurant and a guesthouse for Thai tourists. Meh Dang asks one of the merchants if the hilltribe people still come to dance in the green clearing beyond the market. "I remember we watched dancers, drummers, people from the Karen tribe, I think. They didn't even speak Thai." The merchant tells her they still come, but now they want to be paid in advance. This man, it seems, is their agent. He says, "I know where to find them, if you'd like to see a performance, but I'll have to send someone off to call them, and there is a charge." Other Thai people on the mountain and some of the villagers also want to see the tribal dances. Meh Dang is a clever bargainer. She and the agent bicker and banter about the price of the dancers, the cost of the music, the number of songs. She gives him some money and he tells her to wait for at least half an hour.

While he is gone, we poke around the stalls of jewellery and uncut gems. Shelves terraced around us are stocked with teas from China, tiger balms, and ancient medicines made of ground turtle shell, elephant tusks and snake innards. They will make a woman become pregnant, they will make a man irresistible, they will give strength to those with weak lungs, they will improve intelligence. The intestines of a cobra will cure impotence. Meh Dang has a headache, though, brought on by the car-sickness, and they don't sell aspirin.

Two hours later, after lunch, the hilltribe people come up the mountain in the back of a rust-knawed truck. They talk quietly among themselves in a language neither Chinese nor Thai. They have come out of their forests, these people of the high places, and they walk easily onto the plateau near the mountain's edge, nothing but sky at their backs. Beyond us all, over the other ridges, clouds collapse in long blue-grey sweeps of rain. The younger children of the tribe cluster near the trees, watching their parents and siblings. Small babies are tied to the children's backs with strips of twisted cloth. They stare beyond their sisters' shoulders with the blackest eyes I've ever seen.

The dancers' daily apparel are clothes that we would call costumes: coloured leggings, black quilted jackets embroidered red, blue, green, yellow, tied with silver bells. Chains and rainbow ropes of beads dangle against the women's foreheads and loop down around their chins. Their heads are wrapped in head-dresses, their teeth red-black from chewing betel-nuts. They look so different from Thai people, so much harder and drier. The older women who do not dance have knobby clawed hands. These people are so clearly part of the land they inhabit; they are roots growing into the sun and wind and rain.

Men begin to beat and ring bronze drums. Strange, metallic, unearthly, the music vibrates in the air, shivers into the green and red silence. Someone breathes into a five-tiered bamboo flute. The music doesn't rise but stays with us, echoing itself. First they dance slowly in a rhythm of grace and ritual, arching their fingers away from their open palms. The people around them sing stories I can't understand. They swing from one dance into another, telling the same secrets again and again, but giving nothing away. They keep their faces closed. Bronze words, their words, the low singing of the flute, the language of their footsteps on the ground—these blend into one steady pulse of a life hidden from us, the spectators. They dance as simply as rain falls.

They dance the grass into its own earth, dance it flat and slick, rushing around each other, meeting, falling away, turning in black, bright-edged circles to the ring of bells. They dance until the rain tells them to stop. Then they part quite suddenly, slinging the bronze drums over their shoulders and wrapping the bamboo flutes in old rags. Laughing and flushed now, they scurry towards the old truck with their children in their arms. Fifteen people disappear as abruptly as they arrived. The truck coughs and shudders away, beaten by the rain. Meh Dang rushes towards the market, her purse over her head. I sneak off towards the trees.

The clang of bronze has beaten a soft spot in my skull.

My head feels hollowed, light as eggshell. I walk into the fine-spined conifers—the first I've seen in Thailand—and make my way to the cliffs. The smell of rain and pine reminds me of Canada, but I have no way to connect the reality of that place with this one. Being here takes me a world away from Thailand; North America is even farther. I cannot think about Canada without feeling a quiet fear of snow, forks, suburbs and concrete.

While looking out over the mountains, I notice children creeping up behind me. They come one by one until a group of eight or nine is scattered behind me, hiding behind trees, some with babies slung down their backs. When I call out to them, they edge farther away, skittish as rabbits. Their feet are shoeless and tarred with mud and twigs, but they laugh with each other, presumably at me, the *falang* standing out in the rain. Three or four of them have distended bellies, and their arms and legs are very thin.

Even when the rest have fled, one girl with light brown hair stays behind, crouching in a camouflage of dirty clothes and skin. I do not even realize she is there until I go deeper into the trees. She clutches two small stones and taps them together like the bronze-players of the hilltribe. When I smile at her, she smiles back with a crooked mouth, teeth already rotting in her jaw. I put a few coins into her hand and she bows her thanks to me. I speak to her in Thai but she doesn't understand. She is Chinese. She throws her stones away and scrambles off in the direction of her friends. Running through the trees, she stumbles and falls down with a thud and dry cough. Before I reach her, she has found the dropped coins, wiped her face on her arm and taken off again, faster than before. Her dirty feet wink back at me, then disappear.

I hear Meh Dang. "Kalen! Kalen! Where are you? I don't want to go into the trees! Come here!" I meet her at the edge of the clearing. She grimaces when she sees me, moaning, "How ugly, how ugly." She breaks a twig off a bush and begins to flick caterpillars off my back. "This is why I don't want to go into the trees, you see?" The caterpillars are black and furry, two or three inches long. I lean over and shake half a dozen out of my hair.

WE ARE LEAVING. That is all we can do, because we don't belong here. I can hardly breathe, leaving these hills. I lean out the open window of the car and lose my eyes to the paths, to the ochre steps kicked in the hillsides. Every crevice in the green walls leads somewhere. Everything has a meaning, a name I don't know. The wrap of beads and the arch of the dancers' fingers explained things I couldn't understand. The harvest time for the meagre crops of these plunging fields is a secret. That such hard-boned mountains yield any nourishment at all seems miraculous. I would die in a week here, if lost; I would shrivel into a wrinkled skin and catch in thorns. Snakes would nest in my ribcage.

We slide down, Meh Dang and I, both of us quiet. Our heads are light with the mist, riddled with bamboo. We come away and meet the smoother earth, the one we know. I breathe easier when we leave behind the thin mountain air. Meh Dang hums a song and relaxes on the flat roads. I enter Chiang Rai as though returning to a city I've loved forever. Children here have finished school for the day; they chequer the streets with familiar blue and white uniforms, they swing their book bags like my friends at Nareerat. Their white socks are clean despite the puddles in the street. Every clear face moves in a common language. The familiar scenes of the streets burst open and blow back to me: the entrance to the market is crowded with yellow and blue umbrellas, the shops glow with movement, kindled by the rich colours of cloth and fruit.

My life here has been so easy that the idea of living on Maysalong stuns me.

Thailand has whittled the world into a great sliver and lodged it beneath my skin. I do not think of one country; I think of them all with an unmanageable scope of vision. I'd like to believe—and I sometimes do—that every boundary between people can be crossed, that we are connected to each other by invisible bonds that override distance. My skin stretches over the earth. I think of atlases and remember history and the future in the same moment.

I will not forget the skeleton walking with a pony. I will not forget the beggars or the barefoot children, though I don't know exactly why remembering them matters. Why do I pay such attention to details I cannot alter? Why do I see these things so clearly? Am I here only to witness, amazed one breath and appalled the next?

BACK IN THE WOODEN HOUSE, I am still awake. Meh Dang is sound asleep on the other mattress. I write this in the second-hand light of the moon. Insomnia tonight. Even in the land of frog-song and whispering crickets, there isn't a sound gentle enough to lull me. I'm tired but persistent. Beneath the shadow of the mosquito net, I squint to see my words. It's not the desire to write that keeps me awake, it's my mind, the troops of green-skinned mountains marching behind my eyes, the faces of raw-boned men, hilltribe bronze, children beating stones together. Sleep is not folded between any of those images. I wonder what the children of Maysalong are dreaming right now.

July 30

ON THE WAY BACK to Denchai the bus stops at a roadside market amid pyramids of green coconuts, tables of bananas and large woks of sizzling oil. Hundreds of people have left their cars and motorcycles crammed along the narrow highway. It's a forested area, mostly teak trees, and some kind of party seems to be taking place. Strangers are laughing together; men with long poles and nets are running around. The ceaseless roar of cicadas only adds to the sense of excitement.

"What is everyone doing here?" I ask.

"Oh, they are catching the jakjan."

A man lopes across the highway in long strides, carrying his pole like a javelin-thrower and shaking a plastic bag in the air. "Fifty, I've got fifty!" he calls. Meh Dang laughs. We walk toward a cluster of people around one of the woks. Suddenly I realize what the *jakjan* is. The sprinter shakes his bag and thrusts it open towards the snapping oil. Dozens of stunned cicadas plunge into the wok and sizzle into black crisps. I get goosebumps all over my body and make a strange noise. Meh Dang says to the people around her, "This is new for the falang." They turn to look at me. Everyone smiles and one man makes a joke about Kentucky Fried Chicken. I stare into the wok. The cicadas are about two inches long. When they are done, a young woman scoops them out of the oil with a metal strainer, lets them cool and dishes them out.

And the people eat them. Everywhere around me, people are munching on fried cicadas. Meh Dang takes one and tears it apart, giving me a wing. She pops it into her mouth, makes a bit of a face but swallows. "It was a bit overdone, I think." I am still holding this black chip in my hand, looking at her in disgust. She giggles. "Kalen, it's good luck. And the wing doesn't taste like anything. Try it." As she says this, one of the catches gets loose. A squadron of cicadas flies towards me. I scream and drop my bit of lucky wing while beating the bugs away. I run for the bus. The Thais laugh and slap their knees, Meh Dang howls. She walks towards me, out of breath from guffawing. "Kalen, Kalen, Kalen, forgive me, I didn't mean to scare you." She buys me a cold coconut with its top carved off, a straw sticking out. "Here, drink this. We go back to Denchai now. You don't have to eat jakjan." Another peal of laughter matches the buzz of the cicadas. She gets into the bus, still wiping her eyes. "But it's good luck, you know, to eat them. We all need good luck, don't we? Maybe someday you will need that luck." She winks at me and sits down. Soon the other passengers join us and we leave the insect extravaganza behind.

August 4, 1987

EVERY DAY SOMETHING HAPPENS and I don't have time to write it down. When an event goes unwritten, I think, I will not forget this day, that moment, the words from that laughing mouth. There is so much I haven't written down, and even more that I haven't touched. The days tear away so quickly now. I fear I'll wake one morning and discover I'm old. I will look backwards into the past and know that all the years I lived were only a few long moments, and that I never knew enough. I've called the airline in Bangkok to confirm my flight date, August 19, two days short of a full year. I don't want to go back.

Every roadside, every wild morning journey to Prae, to the market, even pedalling over the bridge in the morning— again and again, I meet stories and pass them by because there is not enough time to spin out the sensations and web them into words. I am too alive and the days are never still.

I ride into the fields and find two women. While they bathe at the well, a blade of grass comes to life and glides onto the stones. The women shriek, the wind blows down from the sky and six sand-coloured dogs lope across the field.

In movements from a dance, the women flay the pearled green snake with sticks. It is five feet long, thick as a sailing line, still and bloody on the stones. The women's long hair slides over their shoulders and into their eyes. The *pasins* they wear blossom vermillion, blue, yellow; the sky behind them bruises purple-grey with rain. When one of the women spears the snake with a stick and swings it over her head, the dogs leap barking into the air, underbellies creamy white. As the snake whips beyond them, they rush after it, growling and snapping their jaws.

All this splendid horror in seconds, in the rice field behind the monastery. The women bend down again to the water. Was the twisting snake real? Did I see it?

Will I remember this sky and the people beneath it? Ajahn Champa was right when she said a year ago (a year! why so fast?) that Thailand would become a dream to me. It already is, but one I live daily. "Canada will soon be real again," she said the other day. Canada. Canada. I push the word over on my tongue. The country of cold rocks. Was I born there?

I believe everything now, take it literally when new market women ask me where I've come from. Without thinking, I answer "the river" or "the school" or "the old temple." I don't even consider another country. This one is enough.

Canada? The word itself is a question now.

August 8

I PREPARE TO LEAVE. I dig through the year's accumulations: the paper, the books, the silk clothes, the silver jewellery, the three sapphires, the letters, gold-trimmed boxes, the elephant-head opium pipe, the magic shoes, the lion carvings, the dried poppies. I am taking Thailand back with me. Two large boxes are already making the voyage by boat. After talking with the Rotary Club and Ajahn Champa, I've been given permission to spend my last five days with Goong and his family in Bangkok. I call my friends in Chiang Mai, Surapong the lawyer in Chiang Rai.

At Nareerat I give a speech during the morning assembly and make jokes about still disliking school uniforms, especially the shoes. Everyone laughs, remembering the two pairs of shoes which curiously disappeared from the hallways this year. I talk about what I've learned in Thailand, who I've become here, how changed I feel. Naturally, words fall short of conveying what I really want to tell them. I cry when I say, "I cannot be sure when I'm coming back." The children and teachers of Nareerat murmur and clap. How many names do I know here? How many people have I seen? The round *chedis* of the temples rise gold against the blue sky of Prae. The palm trees are suddenly remarkable again.

Everything I do in these last days takes on weight. I move slowly, carefully, aware of everything my hands do, mindful of how food tastes, how cold water splashed on my back feels. I am happy, too, to be leaving, though I believe my happiness rises mostly from the glittery dust of excitement. I am invited to suppers, lunches; I go on outings to the rose garden and little country houses owned by Rotary Club members, elegant places with marble floors and rooms adorned by orchids. I spend my lunch hours at school with Siphon, Dewey, Chet, Lin. They have tricked me into eating cicadas. We sing northern songs in the hallways and bang drumbeats on the doors. The teachers and I have a party in the English department staff room, where we eat *som-tam* that's spicy enough to kill scorpions. I regret having needed to sleep in Thailand. I should have been awake constantly, I should have learned more.

I tell myself: Canada is clean and young and wild, there is open space there, more freedom, no one will stare at my white skin. But the other side of my mouth answers that I love them, these people of the green country, in a way I've never loved any other people, even my own. I do not want more space, or even more freedom. I want more *time.*

RAINFALL. RAINSHATTER. Rain rushing out of the purplish clouds in relentless battalions. Light cracks out of heaven in blue-white whips. Leaning from the shop windows, Kwan and Nong Meh stretch their hands into the cold water with squeals of pleasure.

An hour later, the clouds are white again and billow miles into the sky. As I walk into town, my footsteps splash mud on the backs of my legs. Near the outskirts of Denchai, I find the trickling river has grown to a torrent of frothing brown. Whole limbs of trees float by, then a plastic bag, a sodden feather duster. I walk along the steep banks until I find the place where children come to swim. They jump from an overhanging tree into the current, then catch hold of its branches as they float past. With the water roiling along just fast enough to be playful, the children are fearless. A game of tag starts up. Seven little boys metamorphose into undulating water animals, their glossed bodies bobbing in and out of the current. I watch them for a long time, laughing when they slip from the tree or take each other by surprise with the stealth of crocodiles.

The clouds twist higher into the bright sky. A heavy quilt of light covers my face and shoulders. Twice I glimpse a beige, black-striped lizard in the bushes by the river, but it disappears. The houses beside the water are simple wooden shacks surrounded by chickens and dogs. A rooster with an iridescent tail puffs up his red collar of feathers and crows above the roar of the water. The lady who sells roast bananas waves me over and we chat for a while. As always, I buy a bag of cooked *glu-aye kai*. When she realizes I'm leaving in less than a week, she lets out a cry and gives me back my money. "Oh, how sad! Who will buy these bananas now? Who will take pictures of the elephants in Denchai?" She calls her son, a young man I know from the mechanic's shop who once soldered a broken necklace together for me.

The banana lady asks, "Where are you going now, where? My son will give you a ride. You don't have to walk. Where do you want to go?"

"I'm just going for a walk," I explain.

"No, no, the ground is very dirty. Jop will give you a ride."

Instead of protesting, I accept the bananas and the ride, telling Jop I want to go to the swinging bridge. His mother exclaims, "You wanted to walk there! It's ten kilometres away!"

I probably wouldn't have gone all the way there; the sun is already slanting red over the earth and soon it will be dark. But now that Jop will give me a ride, I can easily go to the bridge and return to Denchai before nightfall.

He wheels his motorcycle over from the edge of the house. It's a real motorcycle, not a little scooter. He is obviously proud of this. Once we get out of his mother's view, he speeds down the last part of the paved road. When we reach the fields, I discover he loves splashing through puddles. He apologizes, but I shout over the thunder of the bike, "Mai pen lai! I don't care about the mud!"

"Are you afraid?"

"No!" I yell into his ear, giving him licence. His recklessness does not outweigh his skill, I tell myself whenever the wheels lose contact with the road. We leave Denchai behind, spewing red water and mud as we go. The light is at its best now, brushing the fields and distant blue hills with a velvet hand. The rice is new green in some paddies, ripe red-gold in others. Men with ploughs pulled by water buffalo lumber shin-deep through mud.

When we arrive at the high swinging bridge, the sun is red lava melting behind the mountains. Jop leaves the bike at one side of the river and we walk over together, making the cables swing and squeal by jumping up and down. I lean over the rail to stare into the swollen swirl of water. The river here is always deeper and wider than in Denchai. I've come swimming here with Lin, Deh and Boh.

On the far bank, Jop tells me he once knew a woman who died in this very spot. Snakebite. As we walk down the path, I glance continually into the grass. He laughs. "I am sure a snake will not bite you. Don't worry." Flowers along the bank have opened to the evening's coolness and the air is laced with light perfume. A small violet flower smells like lily of the valley. When we find a wild jasmine plant, Jop tells me not to pick the blossoms because it could bring bad luck. The smell is intoxicating, though, so we stand drinking the air until the mosquitoes drive us away.

When we return to Denchai, Jop asks me if I want to go anywhere else. I direct him to the hillside monastery where I met the Australian monk. It seems so long ago; I can barely remember what we talked about that day, when Thailand was still so hard for me. We leave the noisy bike to cool off a good distance from the monastery and walk into the grounds. The monks are performing their evening chants in the main temple. The Pali rhythms swell into the night air. There is no other sound on earth like this one. Their voices could melt gold. Through the temple windows, we see them inside, the abbot and his monks sitting cross-legged in a wash of candlelight, faces glowing and open above the saffron robes.

We follow the road to the smaller temple, slip our shoes off in silence and enter the high-ceilinged, narrow building. One light shines near the door. Moths and mosquitoes flicker against it, dappling darkness on the far wall. Scenes from *jakata*—the Buddha's past lives—loom from the walls and ceiling. Their dazzling colours defy the shadows. Jop lights some joss sticks and leaves coins in the collection plate by the shrine. We kneel on the floor and *wai* three times to the prince, who, in the candlelight, might be made of real flesh. We leave the temple very slowly, like an old man and woman. We haven't spoken more than monosyllables for an hour. When he drops me off at the shop, he *wais* very formally and leaves without saying a word. It has started to rain again, very lightly. I'm shivering when I go inside.

August 13

PLA AND I SIT OUTSIDE the shop, watching the people come home from work in *songtows* and on bicycles. School children run past us. Pla takes my hand. Her skin is very soft, only a hint of bones, unlike my own hard hand and big knuckles. We've spent every morning and most evenings together since the beginning of the month, trying to fill in the edges of a friendship neither of us has had enough time for. Pla is so often melancholy, unlike any other Thai I know here, but sometimes her solitary moods leave her. Then we wash clothes together, or go for ice-cream, or complain in good humour about the tyranny of Thai men. Right now we just sit watching the evening scurry towards the market-place.

"I'm leaving tomorrow." She knows this, of course, as does almost everyone in Denchai. I still can't quite believe it. When I watch the men across the street unloading rice sacks into Noi's shop, I can't even imagine not being *able* to watch them. The yank of time and place is too much for me: can Canada even exist? The centre of the world is this little town, the kids at the badminton court howling at my weak backhand, Meh Dang hollering, Beed singing to her daughter, Ajahn Champa smiling like a sage. Names flash through my mind, dozens of people's names, then nameless faces I see every day.

Pla lets my hand go and stands up to follow a customer into the shop. She says, "I know you're going tomorrow. And I am sad. I will be lonely again."

This causes a strange physical reaction in me; my heart moves in my chest, or loses its rhythm. Meh Somjit said exactly the same thing to me this morning when I helped her take the clothes off the line.

August 14

THE TEACHERS FROM PRAE have come. Yupa, Sangkaya, Peroontip, Glanjanaa. Ajahn Champa will see me off at the airport in Bangkok. Meh Dang is here, both my families, Beed, all my friends, the Rotary Club members bearing gifts and business cards. There must be almost one hundred people at the train station, all chattering and writing down their addresses and wishing me luck and taking pictures.

My enormous bags are safely stowed away when the whistle blows. Meh Dang is sobbing like a professional mourner. I hug as many people as I can before I have to leave, and the conductor lets me lean out the coach to wave. The wind, the tracks under me, the living heat of the train gathering speed . . . and I am gone. I hear the conductor's voice: "I am scared you will fall." By that time I can't see the station anymore and Denchai has disappeared and I am crying and crying, because it feels like I've lost them, the gentle people.

August 18

MY DAYS IN BANGKOK have slipped down the *klongs*, into the temple courtyards, into last-minute plane ticket confirmations, into a brief chaste visit with Bom (and his girlfriend). Goong, his friends and I had a party tonight, complete with champagne and dancing and a crazy ride through the red-light district of the city. Bangkok had her own way of saying goodbye to me: on a part of the freeway under construction, amid great orange bulldozers and mysterious roads leading off into the dark, we discovered a large elephant, her grey skin turned ivory by the glaring road-lights. Goong said, "That's a ghost elephant, a ghost!" but it looked alive enough to me. A white elephant at midnight. I don't know what the Thai fortune-tellers would say, but that *must* mean good luck.

204

It is past two a.m., already the nineteenth of August, the day of my departure. Having talked all our words away, we have nothing left to do but sit here in the kitchen under the one bald lightbulb, listening to the tiny footsteps of cockroaches. (At first I didn't believe you could hear them, but then Goong showed me how, both of us holding our breath, thinking "hearing hearing hearing" at the same time. It works; they're all over the place.) Finally, after tiring of even this wonderful pastime, we admit we must go to bed. Goong's parents will be here at seven in the morning to take me to the airport.

"So will you come back?" Goong asks.

"Yes, of course I'll come back."

"Do you promise to come back?"

"I have no other choice. What about you? When will you go to Canada again?"

"I don't know, but I will."

"See? It's the same for me." Sadness hangs between us now, and something like regret. But how is that possible, when we've done nothing regrettable? Both of us are suddenly weary.

"What will you dream about tonight?"

I give him a funny look. "I don't know. I never know what I'll dream." Pause. He grins ever so slightly. Raising my eyebrows, I ask, "Do you know what *you're* going to dream about tonight?"

"Of course."

"What?"

"I'm going to dream of Lake Louise and all that snow."

"Are you kidding?"

"No. This is just like the cockroaches! What did you learn in school, anyway?" He laughs. "Before you go to sleep, think out what you want to dream, scene by scene, then say it out loud. If you want to dream in English, say it in English. If you want to dream in Thai, say it in Thai. Then go to sleep, thinking 'dream this' over and over. And you'll dream that dream." He stands up with an air of triumph. I'm still looking at him curiously. "Believe me!" He pulls me up out of my chair and we give each other a hug.

In bed, I think about tomorrow morning. I already know I'm going to use dozens of tissues and wear dark glasses all the way back to Canada. I going to sob myself through half a dozen time zones, over the Pacific, across the world. But I don't want to dream about that; it will be real soon enough. Instead, I think about my school in Prae, the elegant pale green buildings, my impossible dance class, the beat of hilltribe rhythms ringing down the hallways. I think of the sound of the school itself, the music of it, the pulse of students and teachers rushing up and down stairways, murmuring, laughing. I think, Dream this, dream this.

And I do. During the night, I see Ajahn Champa working alone in the English room, cream-white roses on her desk, a breeze coming through the open windows. When she sees me, she smiles and says in Thai, "Do you want to go now?" I dream we walk down the stairs together and out to the morning assembly. A thousand black-haired children are singing in the fields of Nareerat.

Recent Titles from Turnstone Press